Puffin Books

GO! A BOOK OF GAMES

Worried about your party and how you're going to entertain your guests? Your worries are over. Covering the spectrum from silent to riotous, and useful for children of seven upwards, this selection of games will make any party a howling success.

Each game can be adapted to suit most needs. The book is divided into five main sections, based on how much noise and activity the games generate. They range from boisterous outdoor games best played in fields to quiet indoor games needing a bit of peace – the ideal opportunity to catch your breath after a thunderous game of *Fishtails*! With straightforward rules and the minimum amount of props, no party-giver need fear hordes of lively guests.

For five years Philippa Dickinson organized games at the Puffin Club's parties and holidays – so everything in this book has been tried, tested and approved by children themselves.

GO!

A Book of Games

Compiled by Philippa Dickinson

Illustrated by Robin Lawrie

Puffin Books

Puffin Books, Penguin Books Ltd, Harmondsworth, Middlesex, England
Penguin Books, 625 Madison Avenue, New York, New York 10022, U.S.A.
Penguin Books Australia Ltd, Ringwood, Victoria, Australia
Penguin Books Canada Ltd, 2801 John Street, Markham, Ontario, Canada L3R 1B4
Penguin Books (N.Z.) Ltd, 182–190 Wairau Road, Auckland 10, New Zealand

First published 1982

Printed and bound in Great Britain by
Cox & Wyman Ltd, Reading
Photoset in Linotron 202 Plantin by
Rowland Phototypesetting Ltd, Bury St Edmunds, Suffolk

For P.D. and M.R.D.

CONTENTS

ACKNOWLEDGEMENTS

Many of the games in this book are played regularly with groups of boys and girls on Colony Holidays, which is where I learned them. Without that valuable experience this book would not have been possible. My thanks also to Ruth Marshall for her advice and help.

Colony Holidays

Colony Holidays are happy and active holidays for people aged between eight and thirteen, who go away for a week or two with others of the same age; they enjoy playing games, making things, seeing things, exploring, walking, singing and making friends. The holidays are held in big houses (including a couple of castles) all round Great Britain and last for a week or ten days at a time. There are usually between thirty and eighty people on a Colony, with a staff of carefully trained young leaders – students, teachers and others – as well as a trained nurse, catering and domestic staff and a director in overall charge.

The whole organization is overseen by the Council for Colony Holidays for School Children, a non-profit-making trust set up with the support of the Department of Education and Science and the Scottish and Welsh Education Departments.

If you would like to know more about the holidays, please write to:

Colony Holidays
Linden Manor
Upper Colwall
Malvern
Worcs. WR13 6PP

INTRODUCTION

I first came across some of these games when I was sent to Nottingham by the Puffin Club to help organize a Puffin Party for a hundred children. In my ignorance, I was expecting the party to be one of the jelly-and-cake bonanzas of my childhood, with old favourites like *Pass the Parcel*, *Pin the Tail on the Donkey* and *Musical Chairs* thrown in for good measure. I couldn't have been more wrong. Jane and Ruth, both seasoned Puffin Party givers, arrived with a cardboard box containing four blindfolds, three flowerpots, three balls (small, medium and large), two dice, a couple of bars of chocolate, a wad of paper, pencils and not much else. Not a jelly in sight.

Any doubts I might have had about the success of this jelly-less jaunt were dispelled as soon as the guests arrived. I had never seen so many children having so much fun together. These games were completely new to me – exciting to play and, just as important, tremendous fun to watch. There was no need for people to feel bored while waiting for their turn to play, no need for the shy wallflower to hide at the bottom of the garden to avoid *having* to play. There they were, a hundred children, laughing their heads off and having a whale of a time.

Most of the games in this book are for children of seven upwards and can be adapted to suit your needs, depending on how many people you are playing with and how much time you have to fill.

Group Size: Each section begins with games that can be played with only a few people and gradually goes on to games for large groups of twenty or more.

Playing Time: Each game is given a rough estimate of how long you might expect to play it. These tend to be minimum times and are useful if you are planning a party or have a specific time to fill. Have fun!

OUTDOOR GAMES

OUTDOOR GAMES

The games in this section are ideally suited to parks, gardens or woodlands, though they can also be used in a playground. If you are playing in a park or some other large area, you should decide on an area to play in and set rough markers, so that nobody goes too far. There is nothing worse than ending a hiding game and finding that someone is missing, cleverly hiding miles away out of earshot, just like those Japanese soldiers who were still fighting World War II ten years after it had ended.

Make sure that you explain all the rules of a game right at the beginning, as it is extremely difficult to add the vital rule that slipped your mind after everybody has scattered and disappeared behind trees.

Water-pistol Shy

Group size: 2–6

Playing time: 5–10 minutes

Area: small sheltered space

You need: 2 or more water-pistols, 6 empty milk-bottles (or washing-up liquid bottles weighted with a few pebbles), 6 table-tennis balls, a bucket of water

Set up your shy by arranging the milk-bottles in a row and balancing a table-tennis ball on top of each one. Test the range of your water-pistols and mark a firing line a suitable distance from the shy. Fill your water-pistols from the bucket and take it in turns to see how many of the table-tennis balls you can knock off the milk-bottles before your pistol runs out of water. The person who gets the most table-tennis balls off in one go is the winner.

Flowerpots

Group size: 2–8

Playing time: 5–10 minutes

Area: anywhere flat

You need: 6 medium-sized, sturdy flowerpots

Mark out a race-course roughly five metres long. Two people start the race, each of them with three flowerpots, using two to stand on and one to move on ahead. The trick is to move the spare flowerpot just far enough ahead so that you can transfer one foot to it, without moving it so far that you cannot reach back to collect the pot you left behind. Anybody falling off, allowing any part of his body to touch the ground or caught trying to shuffle his pots along has to start again, right from the beginning. The winner is the first person across the finishing line.

If you have lots of people playing, you can use the flower-pots to run a relay race.

Halt!

Group size: 2–10

Playing time: 5–15 minutes

Area: anywhere flat

Two people of roughly similar size stand back to back, as if for a duel. On the word 'Go!' they both start to walk away from each other, in a straight line, until they are told to 'Halt!' They then turn round to face each other and this is when the fun starts! Taking it in turn, they each try to estimate how many strides it will take them to reach their opponent. Each estimate must be lower than the one before. This goes on until one of them feels that there is no way that his opponent can make good her claim. He then challenges her to 'Do it!' She then has to try and reach him, without a run-up, starting from the exact spot where she is standing. If she succeeds, she has won. If she fails, she has lost.

You can play this on either a knock-out or a tournament basis – or just for fun.

Balloon Race

Group size: 2–10

Playing time: 5–10 minutes

Area: anywhere flat

You need: 1 balloon per person

Pour a small amount of water into each balloon before blowing it up and sealing it; then mark out a race-course roughly ten metres long.

Each person is given a balloon and must hold it carefully between his knees – it is *just* possible to walk like this! The first person across the finishing line with his balloon intact is the winner. *Beware:* You must cultivate a gentle waddle for this race; otherwise you run the risk of bursting your balloon and getting disqualified, as well as a wetting!

Keywords

Group size: 3–12

Playing time: 10–20 minutes

Area: wood or scrubland; ideally a path with plenty of cover either side

Choose a storyteller. The storyteller chooses a keyword, like WITCH, and tells the rest of the group. As you all walk along together, the storyteller begins to tell her story, making sure that the keyword comes in frequently. Every time the keyword is used, the rest of the group instantly dive for a hiding-place, leaving the storyteller counting from one to ten. Anybody she can still see when she reaches ten loses a life. The game gets harder as the story goes on, because each time the keyword is used, the storyteller counts to a lower and lower number (nine, eight, seven, etc.), leaving the rest of the group with less and less time to hide. The winner is the person with the fewest lives lost; he takes over the job of storyteller and chooses a different keyword. Great for long walks.

Scavenger Hunt

Group size: 4–12

Playing time: 10–20 minutes

Area: almost anywhere

You need: a scavenger list each, a collecting bag or box each

Scavenger hunts depend on the group of people playing being given a list of objects to collect. There are two basic kinds of scavenger list, though you can always get more complicated if you want to:

1) Simply make a list of ten things for each person to collect. A sample list might be: a beech leaf, a twig, a piece of string, some wool, a sweet paper, a joke, a flower, a pebble, a pencil and an apple. But you can use anything that comes to mind.

2) Give the group a word and tell them to collect one thing beginning with each letter of the word.

The first person back with a completed list of things in his collecting bag or box is the winner.

Lurky

Group size: 5–20 (or more)

Playing time: 20–40 minutes

Area: small clear area, surrounded by plenty of trees, bushes or other cover

You need: a large empty can or a small bucket

Place the can upside-down in a marked-out circle in the centre of your clearing. Choose one person to be Lurky; the others go and hide, while Lurky counts to 100 with her eyes shut. Lurky then has to try and find everybody else; she doesn't actually have to catch them but only to *see* them. When she sees someone, Ben perhaps, she races back to the can, places her foot on it and calls out 'Lurky Ben!' Ben is then Lurky's prisoner and has to stay in prison, near to the can. However, if Ben realizes in time that Lurky has seen him, he should race her to the can and try to kick it away before she has a chance to put her foot on it. He then has time to make his getaway and hide again, while Lurky retrieves the can and puts it back in the circle. The can must be returned to exactly the same spot before Lurky can use it again.

As the game goes on, Lurky will accumulate prisoners who didn't beat her to the can. They can be released at any time (unless Lurky actually has her foot on the can) by a free person running in and kicking the can.

If you have a large group, two Lurkies add to the danger and excitement.

Signals

Group size: 5–20

Playing time: 15 minutes (or more)

Area: small clear area, surrounded by plenty of trees, bushes or other cover

---

Choose one person to be Catcher. Catcher counts to 100 with his eyes shut. He then has to try and find everybody else. Like Lurky in the previous game, he doesn't actually have to catch a Hider; all he has to do is to see her. Once a Hider is spotted, Catcher calls 'See you, Jane!' and Jane is caught. She has to go to the prison – the clear area – or any suitable place and wait to be released. If a Hider sees one or more people in prison, all he has to do is wave to them and they are all released. However, it has to be a fairly conspicuous wave – otherwise the prisoners won't spot it – and there is always the danger of the Catcher seeing the wave too. Wave with caution! With a large group, two Catchers help keep the game moving. The game ends when Catcher has caught all the Hiders, and then somebody else takes over as Catcher. Don't let anyone be Catcher for too long – you can always stop the game and appoint another Catcher.

Witch Doctors

Group size: 6–20 (or more)

Playing time: 5–10 minutes

Area: large open area, preferably grass

Choose someone to be the Witch Doctor. Everybody else scatters, while the Witch Doctor gives chase. If you are caught, you must stand absolutely still, legs apart, with your arms held out on either side. You are stuck like that until another person being chased by the Witch Doctor releases you by diving between your legs. They have to be quick at this and you have to be fairly nippy getting away as the Witch Doctor will be on the look-out for people slowed up by either releasing or being released. The game ends after ten minutes, or when the Witch Doctor has caught everybody, and another Witch Doctor is chosen. You cannot be actually caught while you are between someone's legs, but it is not a

good idea to hang about catching your breath there, as all the Witch Doctor has to do is hover nearby until you emerge and catch you on your feet again.

Skinning the Snake

Group size: 8–20 (or more)

Playing time: 5–10 minutes

Area: flat grassy space

Divide the group into equal teams. Each team stands in a line, front to back, legs wide apart, allowing a fair bit of space between teams. Everybody in each team bends over and reaches back with their right hands through their own legs (except for the last person in each team). They also reach forward with their left hands and hold on to the right hand of the person in front of them (except for the first person in each team). It is absolutely essential that the *right* hand goes backwards through the legs and the *left* hand goes forwards. Each team is now in an extremely contorted position – which gets worse as the game goes on! On the word 'Go!' the person at the back end of each team goes down on his knees and crawls forward through the rest of the team's legs, without letting go of the hand he is holding. As soon as he is through the legs of the person in front of him, she, still holding on to his hand and the hand of the person in front of her, gets down on her knees and follows the last person through the team's legs. And so on, until the whole of the team has passed through and emerged at the front, untwisted. It is important to move slowly and gently because any team that breaks hands at any point is out. Also, anybody who raises a leg off the ground to make it easier for a team member to pass through disqualifies his team. The first team out at the front wins.

Leggoals

Group size: 8–14

Playing time: 10–15 minutes

Area: flat open space

You need: a football or similar sized ball

Stand in a circle with your legs apart. Everybody's legs should be roughly the same distance apart, feet just touching the feet of the people on either side. Give the ball to one person to start. The idea of this game is to try and hit the ball between the legs of one of the other people in the circle, while trying to prevent them doing the same to you. If the ball goes through your legs, that is a goal. The first person to let through three goals has lost. You should use your fists to hit the ball, knocking it *down* and between somebody's legs. Your feet must not move from the spot and you must not bend your knees. Anybody spotted squatting or using anything except their fists to protect their goal deserves dire punishment.

A word of warning: Since all heads are down, bending over to protect the goalmouths, it is important to keep the ball on the ground and not to hit it up at all as you run the risk of hitting somebody painfully in the face with a high-speed ball.

Dragons

Group size: 8–20 (or more)

Playing time: 5–10 minutes

Area: open, flattish space

You need: a blindfold for each dragon

Get into groups of between four and six. Each group should choose a dragon Head, who will be blindfolded. The rest of the group line up behind the dragon Head, each with their

hands on the shoulders of the person in front. The person immediately behind the Head is the Brain and can direct the Head only by pressure on the Head's left or right shoulder. The Brain is not allowed to speak to the Head. The rest of the group behind the Brain are the Body and the last person in the line is the Tail. When every dragon is lined up and ready to go, the Brains can start their Heads moving, with their Tails tagging on behind. The idea is for each Brain to steer his Head so that the Head can catch hold of another dragon's Tail. He has also got to be aware of what is happening to his own Tail and try to keep it away from the jaws of another dragon. If a Head catches the Tail of another dragon, then the dragon she has caught is out. If a dragon breaks at all, it is also out, so keep a firm hold! The last dragon left at the end is victorious.

Crows and Cranes

Group size: 8–20

Playing time: 10 minutes

Area: flat open space

You need: 6 stumps or objects to mark corners and lines

Mark out two base lines and a centre line approximately five metres long, leaving roughly fifteen metres from the centre line to each of the base lines.

Choose one person to be Caller and divide the rest into two equal teams, each team standing back to back with the other team along the centre line. One team are the Crows, the other the Cranes. The Caller stands to one side and calls either 'Crows' or 'Cranes'. To keep the teams guessing, the Caller can take some time getting past the 'Cr . . . Cr . . . Cr . . .'

bit. If he calls 'Crows!', all the Crows make a mad dash for their base line, with the Cranes in hot pursuit. If a Crane catches a Crow before she reaches the safety of the Crow base line, then the Crow has to give the Crane a piggyback all the way back to the centre line. If 'Cranes!' is called, the Cranes run for their base line and the Crows give chase. You could count points for this game or give everybody three lives, but it is probably best just played for fun.

Skylark

Group size: 10–20 (or more)

Playing time: 20–30 minutes

Area: flat open space

You need: 4 stumps or objects to mark 4 corners, a tennis ball, a whistle

Mark out a rectangular area roughly twice as long as it is wide, say twenty-five by fifty metres, using the stumps.

Divide the group into two teams and choose a Referee. One team, the Throwers, line up along one end of the area, while the other team, the Catchers, scatter themselves around inside the area. One of the Throwers hurls the tennis ball as high up into the air as she can, making sure that the ball will come back down inside the area. If the ball falls outside the area, the throw must be taken again. As soon as the ball has been thrown, all the Throwers make a dash for the far end of the area. The Catchers are powerless to stop them until a Catcher has the ball. As soon as the ball is caught, the Referee blows the whistle and the Catchers can start tagging Throwers. Throwers who are caught before they reach the end line are out, but any Thrower reaching the end line safely wins a point for his team. When all the Throwers are either safe or out, they start again with another Thrower hurling the ball into the air. Gradually the Throwers will be whittled down until they are all out. The Referee makes a note of the points they have scored and then the teams change places. The team with the most points wins.

Jockeys

Group size: 10–20

Playing time: 10–15 minutes

Area: flat grass

You need: a tennis ball or some other small, easily seized object

Choose one person to be Caller; the others divide into pairs, roughly by height and weight, though this is not essential. The pairs stand in a circle facing inwards, with one half of each pair, the Jockey, perched piggyback on his long-suffering partner's back. The tennis ball is placed in the centre of the circle. The Caller shouts 'Left!' or 'Right!' and the Jockeys leap off their partners' backs and race round the outside of the circle in the direction that was called until they get back to their partners. As soon as a Jockey has got back to his partner, he dives through her open legs into the centre of the circle, making a grab for the tennis ball. The Jockey who gets the ball scores a point for his pair. The Jockeys then change places with their partners, who in turn have a go at being Jockeys. The game goes on until one pair reaches five points, or until everybody collapses from weak knees.

Fifteen Passes

Group size: 10–20

Playing time: 10–20 minutes

Area: open space

You need: a football

Divide the group into two teams, trying to get an even mix of size and ability. Toss a coin to decide who starts. The team who win the toss have to try and pass the ball by hand between their own members fifteen times. The ball must not touch the ground. The other team try to intercept the ball as it goes from one to another. If they manage to intercept the ball, they then try to reach a total of fifteen passes themselves. You cannot run with the ball. As soon as the ball is passed to you, you must stand still until you have passed it on to someone else. You cannot knock the ball out of someone's hands.

Sounds easy? It isn't, especially when you are getting close to your side's total of fifteen passes!

Gap-stopping

Group size: 10–20

Playing time: 10–15 minutes

Area: flat open area

Choose someone to be Tapper and get the others into a close circle facing inwards, with shoulders nearly touching. Tapper walks round the outside of the circle and touches somebody on the shoulder. The instant Tapper touches somebody, he turns and runs back around the circle the way he has come. The person Tapper has touched leaves her place and runs round the outside of the circle in the opposite direction (the same way Tapper was walking before touching her). When their paths cross on the opposite side of the circle, Tapper should run outside the girl he has touched, since he has the element of surprise in his favour. This avoids a head-on collision. The first one back to the gap left by the girl fills it while the other one is left to become Tapper and choose another victim. Anybody stuck with being Tapper three times in succession should be let off and somebody else chosen.

Prisonerball

Group size: 10–20 (or more)

Playing time: 15–30 minutes

Area: flat open space

You need: 6 stumps or objects to mark lines and corners, a football

Mark out an area roughly ten by twenty metres and mark a half-way line dividing the rectangle into two squares, each ten metres square.

Divide into two equal teams, each team standing inside one of the squares. Toss a coin to decide who starts. Let's say the Black Shirts are playing the White Shirts and the Black Shirts win the toss, getting the first throw of the ball. (Both teams can move about as much as they like, but they must remain inside their squares.) The Black Shirt with the ball has to throw it into the White Shirts' square, trying to hit one of them anywhere on the body except the head. The White Shirts, of course, all leap around like mad, trying to avoid

being hit. If one of them is hit, he becomes a Prisoner and must retire to the base line behind the Black Shirts' square. If the Black Shirt's throw is feeble and doesn't hit anyone, then a White Shirts' player can pick up the ball as soon as it has either touched the ground or gone over a line. That White Shirts' player can either have a go at hitting a Black Shirt or she can pass the ball to another, better positioned White Shirt. If, by a particularly skilful or lucky throw, more than one person is hit, they are all Prisoners.

Gradually, both sides will end up with Prisoners behind their base lines, which adds another twist to the game. Whenever the ball goes over the base line, either because it has gone straight through the square without hitting anybody or because it has been deliberately passed over to the Prisoners from their own team, a Prisoner can use it to attack his opponents from behind. If he manages to throw the ball and hit an opponent, then he is released and can go back to his team's square, while the person he hit is made a Prisoner and has to join her fellow Prisoners behind the opposite base line. The only exception to this is when the ball crosses the base line *after* having hit someone, as it then belongs to the team in the square. If the ball crosses a side line, it belongs to the team whose side line it crossed. If the ball crosses the base line when there are no Prisoners, it belongs to the team whose base line it crossed.

The skill in this game comes from the agility needed to avoid the ball as it cannons into your square and the speed needed to catch the opposing team unawares, so it is essential to keep the ball moving fast.

Line and Fielders

Group size: 10–20 (or more)

Playing time: 20 minutes

Area: flat open space

You need: a ball

Divide into two equal teams, one to be the Line, the other to be the Fielders. The Fielders scatter themselves round the area while the Line stand in a close queue, squashed up to each other as tightly as they can. The person at the head of the Line has the ball and throws it as far as he can in any direction he feels like, ideally away from the Fielders. As soon as the ball has left his hand, he zooms as fast as he can round and round the Line (which is why they all have to squash up tight); each complete run round the Line gives his team a point. Meanwhile, the Fielders all make a mad dash for the ball. The first Fielder there picks up the ball and the rest form a line behind her. She passes the ball backwards over her head to the Fielder behind her, he passes it over his head to the next and so on down the line to the last Fielder. As soon as the last Fielder has the ball in his hand, he shouts 'Stop!' and the Line runner must stop running. The exhausted runner goes to the back of the Line and the next Line player throws the ball. When all the Line have thrown the ball, the teams change roles. The team with the most points at the end wins.

Continuous Cricket

Group size: 10–20 (or more)

Playing time: 40 minutes or more

Area: large open playing-field

You need: a ball (a tennis ball if you are all feeling very energetic, a small hand ball if you are not), 5 cricket stumps, a cricket bat

Set up three stumps as the Batter's wicket, as in ordinary cricket. Knock in another stump roughly ten metres in front of the wicket for the Bowler. Knock in the last stump roughly ten metres to one side of the Batter's wicket.

Divide into two equal teams, one to be Batters, the other to be Fielders. The Fielders choose a Bowler and a Wicket-keeper (who can be changed at any time during the innings) and the rest scatter round the field. The Batters decide on the order in which they are going to bat and send their first Batter in, armed with the cricket bat, to stand in front of the wicket and wait for a ball to be bowled to him. The rest of the Batters stay, in batting order, somewhere behind the wicket, out of the way but not too far away.

The Bowler bowls underarm (no Test Match tricks here!) at the wicket. The ball must bounce once before it reaches the wicket. It must not bounce more than once, nor can it go so wide that the Batter hasn't a hope of reaching it. If the ball does anything other than just bounce once before reaching the wicket, it is a no-ball; the Batter cannot be bowled out and does not have to hit it. If, however, the Batter chooses to hit a no-ball, it then counts as a fair ball and he can be out from it.

A Batter can be out in a number of ways. He can be bowled or caught in the usual way, hit his own wicket with the bat or intentionally hit the ball behind the wicket. If the ball *accidentally* goes behind the wicket, he is not out, but he may not run. There is no leg-before-wicket rule in this game, but obviously you use your sense about this. If you see a Batter deliberately putting his legs in the path of the ball, you can declare him out.

The Batter must hit the ball forward. As soon as he has hit a ball, he makes a dash for the side stump, where he must touch his bat just beyond the stump before running back to his wicket. Each time he gets back to his wicket, having completed a run, he scores a point for his team. There is no limit to the number of runs that can be scored off one ball. However, in the meantime, the Fielders are rushing madly after the ball, trying to get it back to the Bowler as fast as they can. As soon as the Bowler has got the ball back in her hands, she can bowl it again at the wicket, regardless of whether the Batter is back from his run. So, if the Batter hit the ball feebly and it didn't go very far, the Fielders should be able to get it back to the Bowler while the poor Batter (who *has* to run) is still on his way back from the side stump, leaving a nice, unprotected wicket to bowl at. There is also the undeniable fact that this game can be extremely wearing for the Batter: the more runs he scores, the more tired his legs get, the slower he runs and the easier he is to bowl out. It is very important that the Bowler should keep up the pressure and bowl again as soon as she has the ball.

As soon as a Batter is out, the next Batter must rush in and take the bat from him because the Bowler doesn't pause for a change of Batter. The slightest hesitation by the Batters could leave the wicket exposed for a crucial moment and the new Batter could be bowled out before she is in. This is why it is important to know the batting order from the beginning.

When all the Batters are out, the teams change sides. The team with the most points at the end wins.

Platters

Group size: 10–20

Playing time: 10–20 minutes

Area: flat open space

You need: 3 or 4 tin cans (the larger the better), a tennis ball

---

Divide the group into two equal teams, one Throwers, one Taggers. Stack the cans on top of each other. The Throwers stand in a line some distance away from the pile of cans, the first Thrower with the tennis ball in her hand. She chucks the ball at the pile of cans and tries to knock it down. As soon as the cans fall, she dashes up to the pile and rebuilds it while the rest of the Throwers scatter. In the meantime, the Taggers retrieve the ball and try to hit as many Throwers as they can with it. The Thrower rebuilding the cans cannot be hit. The Taggers score one point for each Thrower they hit and the Throwers score three points for each time the pile of cans is knocked down and rebuilt. As soon as the cans are back where they started, the Taggers must stop and the next Thrower has the ball. When all the Throwers have had a throw, the teams swap roles. The team with the most points wins.

Scots and English

Group size: 10–20 (or more)

Playing time: 20 minutes or more

Area: large flat open space

You need: 6 clearly identifiable tokens for each team (6 blue socks and 6 red socks, for instance), 6 cricket stumps

Mark out a very large rectangular playing area with a stump at each corner and two stumps marking the centre line across it. Place the six blue socks at even intervals along one base line and the red socks along the other.

Divide into two teams of roughly equal cunning and guile. The Blues have the part of the playing area with the red socks along the base line and the Reds have the blue socks behind them. The Blues have to try and get the blue socks back from the Reds' prison and the Reds have to try and rescue the red socks from the Blues' prison. The moment a Blue crosses the centre line into the red area, she can be caught by a Red. If she is caught by a Red, she becomes a prisoner and must be escorted by the Red back to the red prison. The same happens to the Reds in the blue area. Once the Red has caught a Blue, he cannot catch another one until he has escorted his first catch back to the red prison. The prisoner must not struggle or try to escape once she has been caught.

If the Blue is cunning and manages to reach the red prison without being caught, she can take either a blue sock or another imprisoned Blue back with her. She cannot take both. Once the Blue has got either a sock or a rescued Blue with her, she has a safe conduct and can return across the red area to the blue area.

Meanwhile, the Reds are trying the same kinds of raids into the blue area. It is a good idea for both sides to divide themselves into raiders and defenders, with the raiders going after their tokens and rescuing captured team-mates while the defenders protect their prison against raiding parties from the opposing team. The first team to get all their tokens back to their own base line has won.

Generals

Group size: 10–20 (or more)

Playing time: 30 minutes or more

Area: woods, bushes, plenty of cover

You need: 1 small bit of paper for each player

Divide the bits of paper into two equal armies and label each army as follows: *General 10, Brigadier 9, Colonel 8, Major 7, Captain 6, Lieutenant 5, Sergeant 4, Corporal 3, Private 2* and *Spy 1*. If you are less than twenty people, leave out some of the middle ranks, but be sure to keep both the General and the Spy. If you are more than twenty, double up on some of the middle ranks. Don't double up on the General or the Spy unless you are playing with a huge group.

Divide into two armies and find some method of distinguishing between them: one army can roll up its sleeves or trouser-legs, while the other paints its faces with blue stripes. Each army shuffles its bits of paper and deals them out so that everybody has one and knows his rank and power number. Both armies then choose their own secret base at some distance from the other – and now battle can begin. Each army is trying to capture the other army's General in order to win. However, since the General is the most powerful person in the army and can only be caught by the weakest member of the opposite army, the Spy, this calls for a lot of cunning and some nifty tactical planning. In order to catch a member of the opposite army, you simply walk up to him, tag him and say 'Challenge'. He then has to tell you what rank he is and you have to tell him your rank. The highest rank wins the challenge (except when the Spy meets the opposing General), takes the loser prisoner and marches him back to the secret base. If two equal ranks challenge each other, neither is made prisoner.

Prisoners can be released from the enemy base, but only by a free soldier slipping past the guard, if there is one, and touching the prisoner. The prisoner is then free and must make his way back to his base before setting out again.

Gradually, as the game goes on, you will begin to identify certain people with certain ranks and it becomes a process of elimination to discover who is the enemy General and who is the enemy Spy. Once you have spotted the other General, you can send your Spy out to capture him. But beware! Who knows whether the enemy have managed to work out who your Spy is and are waiting in ambush to pounce?

Jug-handle He

Group size: 12–20 (or more)

Playing time: 10–20 minutes

Area: open space

Choose one person to be He and one person to be chased. Everybody else gets into pairs and links arms with their partners. Your free hand should be placed on your hip so that your elbow sticks out at the side like a jug-handle. Form a circle, leaving roughly a metre space between each pair.

The game begins with He chasing his victim all over the place, in and out and round about the circle. The victim can run anywhere but should be careful not to get too far away from the safety of the circle. If He catches his victim, they swap roles and the victim becomes He instead. At any time, the victim can gain safety by linking arms with somebody's jug-handle, forcing the other person of the pair to leave and be chased by He. Since this arm-linking can happen fast and furiously, it is vitally important that everybody in the circle should keep a careful eye on what is going on, just in case they suddenly get forced out into the path of a rampaging He.

Tierce

Group size: 12–20 (or more)

Playing time: 10–20 minutes

Area: open space

Choose two people, one to be Tierce, one to be Catcher. The rest of the group get into pairs and stand in a wide circle, one member of each pair standing immediately behind his partner, facing into the centre of the circle. Catcher must stay inside the circle, while Tierce hovers outside the circle. Tierce has to try and dash into the circle and stand in front of one pair without being caught by the Catcher. If Tierce manages this, the back member of the pair he has chosen instantly becomes Tierce. Catcher can only catch Tierce inside the circle and Tierce must actually have come to a halt in front of his chosen pair to avoid being caught. If Catcher does manage to catch Tierce, they change places.

Cat and Mouse

Group size: 20 or more

Playing time: 10–15 minutes

Area: flat open space

You need: a whistle

Divide the group into equal teams, trying to get roughly as many people in a team as there are teams, like four teams of five, six teams of six and so on. Line the teams up in rows facing you and tell them to hold their arms straight out to the sides. They should just be able to touch the outstretched fingers of their neighbours on either side. When that is done, tell them to turn through ninety degrees, arms still stretched out, so that they make lines from back to front instead. Here too, they should just be able to touch the fingertips of their team-mates on either side.

When the whistle blows, they must all turn back to their original position. When you blow the whistle again, they turn through ninety degrees again. Each time the whistle goes, they should turn from one position to the other. Practise this a few times to make sure that everybody knows what they're doing.

Choose two people, preferably from the end of rows, and make one Cat and the other Mouse. Give Mouse a few moments' start and then let Cat give chase. Both must run between the rows of people and neither is allowed to break through a line between outstretched hands. If Cat catches Mouse, they change roles.

You, as Whistle-blower, have control over the course that Cat and Mouse run through – and this is where the fun starts! If you see Cat getting close to Mouse, you can blow the whistle, everybody turns through ninety degrees – and suddenly the rows are running in a different direction! Equally, if you see Mouse evading Cat too easily, you can blow the whistle, change the direction of the rows – and Mouse suddenly finds himself in danger, with an avenging Cat bearing down on him along a row that had not existed a moment before! Or you can blow the whistle at any time, just to keep Cat and Mouse on their toes. When your first Cat and Mouse have had enough, choose two more people to have a go and somebody else to be Whistle-blower.

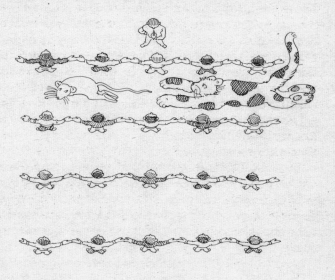

NOISY INDOOR GAMES

NOISY INDOOR GAMES

These are active games, best suited to a school hall, a playroom or a big room cleared of valuable objects. They involve a certain amount of rushing about and generate a fair bit of noise, so shouldn't be played too close to sleeping babies or aged aunts.

Don't announce any of the games as being noisy – they'll get noisy enough on their own. In fact, you can sometimes announce them as just the opposite to add a touch of bewilderment to the jollity.

Make sure that you have enough space cleared in your room; otherwise you might find your racers smashing into a row of spectators or a wall at the end of a race-course.

You can also play several of these games outdoors, preferably on a flat, open area of grass.

Jumble Race

Group size: 3–20

Playing time: 5–10 minutes

Area: room for a short race-course

You need: old clothes, the older and weirder the better, with 1 of each type of garment for each player (or each team)

Mark out your race-course, roughly ten metres long, and place each pile of clothes at even intervals along the end line.

Line everybody up along the starting line of the course and tell them the order in which the clothes must be collected – hat, scarf, shirt, jacket, gloves, skirt, boots – and shout 'Go!' Everybody hops off for their pile of clothes, puts on the hat and hops back to the starting line. As soon as they are back to the line, they instantly turn round and hop back for the next garment. If any garment falls off, they must stop and put it back on again. The first person back to the starting line wearing all his clothes, looking like a walking jumble sale, wins.

If you have a large group, you can play this as a relay race, which is easier, since each racer only has to cope with one garment at a time.

Are You There?

Group size: 4–20 (or more)

Playing time: 5–10 minutes

Area: clear floor space

You need: 2 blindfolds, 2 rolled-up newspapers

Choose two people to play and get them to lie face downward on the floor, facing each other and holding each other's left hand. Blindfold both of them and put a rolled-up newspaper in their right hands. Taking it in turns, one of them asks 'Are you there?' The other one has to answer 'Yes' and instantly twist herself out of the way. At the same time, the person who asked the question has to try and tap her on the head or shoulders with his newspaper, which isn't nearly as easy as it sounds. He gets one attempt to tap her and then it is her turn to ask the question. The first person to score three taps wins. Then two more people can have a go.

Left-handed people should be paired together and hold the newspapers in their left hands.

The Minute Game

Group size: 4–20 (or more)

Playing time: 20–40 minutes

Area: almost anywhere

You need: a prepared list of subjects, either a bell, a whistle or a hammer, a stop-watch or a watch with a second hand

Make a list of twenty or so subjects for people to talk about. The subjects can be as serious or as silly as you like, ranging from *My Teddy Bear* to *The Prime Minister*.

Taking it in turns, each person has a chance to speak for exactly one minute about the subject you give him. If you have a large group, divide them up into roughly equal teams and have one person from each team play at a time. The person who is given the subject must speak on that subject for one minute without *wandering*, *repetition* or *hesitation*. If one of the other players feels that the speaker has either wandered off the subject he was given, repeated a word or hesitated, she can challenge by holding up her hand. As soon as a challenge is made, you stop the clock or make a note of how much of the minute has gone. The challenger then has to justify her challenge. If you feel that her challenge is correct, she gets a point for herself or her team and has to carry on with the subject herself as soon as you start the clock again. If the challenge is thought to be incorrect, the person who was challenged gets a point for himself or his team, keeps the subject and must continue on that subject until the minute is up or until he is challenged again. The person speaking when the minute is up wins another point. The person, or team, with the most points when you have finished your list of subjects is the winner.

Traffic Lights

Group size: 4–15 (or more)

Playing time: 5–10 minutes

Area: large clear space

You need: 3 paper circles – 1 red, 1 yellow or amber, 1 green

Choose a Traffic Controller, who is given the paper circles. The rest of you form a line close together – or two lines if there are a lot of you. The Traffic Controller holds up one of the circles, calling out its colour at the same time. When 'Green' is called, everybody in the line must step forward one pace; when 'Red' is called, they must all go back a pace; for 'Amber' they must just stand still. Anybody making a mistake is out. If the Traffic Controller starts fairly slowly, she can gradually build up speed, which is guaranteed to cause chaos and confusion. The last person left in is the winner.

Clapping Hot and Cold

Group size: 4–20 (or more)

Playing time: 5–10 minutes

Area: a room with a door

Send someone outside. The rest of you decide on some fairly simple thing that you want her to do, like moving a plant from the window to the table, taking someone's shoes off or standing on the table. Call her back in again and don't say anything. She starts moving about the room and you help her get close to the thing that you want her to move or whatever by clapping your hands quietly when she moves in the wrong direction and clapping loudly when she moves in the right direction. When you have actually got her to the right place, it becomes a game of trial and error as you guide her with quiet and loud claps until she has performed the task correctly. When she's done it, choose someone else to go outside while the rest decide on a new task.

The Mummy Game

Group size: 4–20

Playing time: 5–10 minutes

Area: clear space

You need: a roll of soft toilet-paper for each pair, a whistle

Get into pairs. Each pair has a roll of toilet-paper and must decide before the game starts which of them is going to be wrapped up. That decided, the Judge blows the whistle and the Wrapper sets to wrapping his partner up with the toilet-

paper. She must use the whole roll and try to make her partner look as much like an Egyptian mummy as possible. After a set time-limit, like three minutes, has passed, the Judge blows the whistle and tries to decide which is the best mummy.

A messy game but a great end to a party.

Scarecrow

Group size: 4–20

Playing time: 5 minutes

Area: room for a short race-course

You need: old clothes as for the *Jumble Race*

Mark out your race-course, roughly ten metres long, and place each player's pile of clothes at even intervals along the end line.

Divide your players into two or more teams and ask each team to choose a Scarecrow. The Scarecrows stand with their teams at one end of the course with the piles of clothes at the other end. When you shout 'Go!', the first player from each team runs to her pile of clothes, brings back one garment and must put it on the Scarecrow properly – buttons done up, hooks fastened – before the next player can run for another garment. The first and best-dressed Scarecrow and his team win.

Fishtails

Group size: 5–20 (or more)

Playing time: 5 minutes (or more)

Area: large clear space

You need: a half-sheet of newspaper (cut into a fish shape if you feel like it) for each person, with about 120 cm of string or cotton attached to a short edge (through the fish's nose)

Attach the loose end of a string through a belt or round your waist so that the newspaper just lies flat on the ground behind you when you are standing up. When everybody's tails are firmly attached, the game can start. On the word 'Go!' you must try and stamp on as many tails as you can,

while trying to keep your own tail safe from everybody else's feet. You must not touch your own tail, tuck it up or interfere with it in any way. If your tail is stamped on, you are out and must leave the game. The last person left with his tail intact is the winner.

Eating Chocolate

Group size: 5–20 (or more)

Playing time: 10–15 minutes

Area: clear floor space

You need: a knife, a fork, a paper plate, a hat, a scarf, a die and an 8 oz. bar of milk chocolate for each group of (up to 15) people

If you have a large group of people, divide them into smaller groups of roughly the same size and with not more than about fifteen people in each. Each group sits in a circle, with the knife, fork, hat and scarf by the chocolate bar (still in its paper wrapper) on a plate in the centre of the circle. Everybody takes it in turn round the circle to throw the die and then pass it on to the next person. When someone throws a six, she dives into the middle of the circle, puts on the hat and the scarf, picks up the knife and fork and starts attacking the bar of chocolate, hoping to be able to cut off enough to eat. She must not use her hands directly on the chocolate. She can use only the knife and fork even to unwrap the bar. She stays in the centre of the circle, eating as much of the chocolate as she can, until someone else throws a six. When this happens, she stops, takes off the hat and scarf and returns to her place, while the person who threw the six dives into the circle, puts on the hat and the scarf and gets going on the bar of chocolate with the knife and fork. The game continues until the last bits of chocolate have been eaten.

Stealing Apples

Group size: 8–20 (or more)

Playing time: 5–10 minutes

Area: clear space in a room with a door

You need: an apple or a tennis ball

Choose a Thief, who is banished outside the door until you are ready for him. Everybody else sits in a wide circle with the apple in the middle. Choose a Farmer and keep quiet about it. Call the Thief back into the room. The Thief has to get into the middle of the circle, take the apple and get away without the Farmer catching him. The Thief can get into the circle between any two people but *must* leave the circle by the same gap. The Farmer cannot move to catch the Thief until the Thief has actually touched the apple. Of course, the Thief has absolutely no idea who the Farmer is until he touches the apple, so woe betide him if he happens to enter the circle next to the angry Farmer! If the Farmer catches the Thief, the Thief has to go out again while a new Farmer is chosen. If the Farmer fails to catch the Thief, the Farmer goes out to be the Thief next time. A Thief can have three attempts at stealing the apple and then another person should be chosen.

Seat Circle

Group size: 10–20

Playing time: 5 minutes

Area: clear space

Get everybody to form a circle and then make a ninety-degree turn to the right so that everyone is facing the back of the person in front. Get them to stand as close as possible to each other, making a really tight circle. On the word 'Go!' everybody gently begins to sit down. If you've got the circle tight enough, you will all end up sitting, if a bit precariously, on the knees of the person behind you. If someone goes down faster than the rest or gets an attack of wobbly knees, the circle collapses.

If your circle is feeling particularly clever and can manage to sit down and stay there, try getting them to walk forward round the circle. If they can manage *that* without collapsing, try getting them to walk backwards!

A skilful game with hysterical moments.

Chinball

Group size: 10–20 (or more)

Playing time: 5 minutes

Area: clear space

You need: a tennis ball for each team

Divide into small teams of the same size and sit down in tight rows. The tennis balls start at the top of each team and have to be passed down the lines, clenched tightly between chin and shoulder or chest. No hands or teeth may be used and any team fumble-chinned enough to drop the ball has to start again from the top. The first team to manage to pass the ball chin-to-chin the whole way down the line wins. It is surprising how difficult it can be to chin-pass a ball when both you and your neighbour are in fits of giggles!

Matchbox

Group size: 10–20 (or more)

Playing time: 5 minutes

Area: open space

You need: an empty matchbox with the drawer removed for each team

Divide the group into equal teams and sit the teams in close lines. Start the empty matchbox cover at the top of each team by fitting it carefully on to the nose of the first person. The next person in each line has to wedge her nose carefully into the other end of the matchbox case and gently remove it from the first person's nose. The next person in the line then does the same – and so on, down the line, until the matchbox cover has reached the last person in the line. If the matchbox is dropped, it has to start again at the top of the line. The first team to get their matchbox cover to the end of their line wins.

General Post

Group size: 10–20 (or more)

Playing time: 10–15 minutes

Area: large open space

You need: chairs for all but 1 person, a list of about 6 towns prominently displayed on the wall

Arrange the chairs in a circle. Everybody but you sits on a chair. Go round the circle dividing the group equally into towns, so that three people become Birmingham, three Manchester, three Liverpool, and so on. Don't forget to include yourself. You then announce that you are going to send a letter from one town to another, say from Manchester to Liverpool. All the people called either Manchester or Liverpool have to leave their chairs and *walk* to another chair. While they are doing this, you nip in and sit on an empty chair, which will leave one person chairless in the middle of the circle, who then has to start again. Of course, it isn't as simple as that because there are a variety of things that can be sent from place to place, some of which travel faster than others. So, to send a letter, everybody must *walk*, for a postcard they must *hop*, for a parcel they must *crawl* and for a telegram they must *run*.

Slap Penny

Group size: 10–20 (or more)

Playing time: 5–10 minutes

Area: clear space

You need: 10 coins or buttons for each team, 2 chairs (or bowls) for each team

Divide into teams of the same size (five to eight people). Each team sits in a row, cross-legged, with a chair (or bowl) at each end. Put ten coins for each team on the chairs at one end. On the word 'Go!' the first person in the team picks up a coin from the chair and places it on the palm of his up-turned left hand. He then slaps the coin on to the palm of his right hand and, from there, slaps it on to the left palm of the team-mate on his right. She slaps the coin on to her right palm, then on to her neighbour's left palm, and so on down the team. The last person in the team receives the coin on her left palm, slaps it on to her right and then on to the chair at her end. Meanwhile, the first person in the team has started another coin off down the line as soon as the first one has left him.

The coins must not be held in the fingers, gripped or dropped. If anybody is butter-palmed enough to do any of these things, the coin must go back and start from the top again.

This game sounds extremely simple. However, transferring the coin from one person to another needs a quick flick of the wrist and can be tricky. The first team with all ten coins on their chair at the end wins.

Knee-tapping

Group size: 10–20 (or more)

Playing time: 10 minutes

Area: clear space

You need: chairs for everybody, a rolled-up newspaper fastened with sellotape

Arrange the chairs in a circle and ask everybody to sit on one. Take your chair into the centre of the circle. With the newspaper knee-tapper in your hand, wander around the inside of the circle until you spot a suitable victim. Tap him gently on the knee with the knee-tapper and race back to the centre of the circle, where you leave the knee-tapper on the seat of your chair. If the knee-tapper falls off your chair, you must go back and put it on the seat properly.

As soon as you tap your victim's knee, he leaps out of his chair and chases you to the centre of the circle. He picks up the knee-tapper from the chair and must try to tap you with it before you can get back to his chair. If he gets you, he can have his chair back and you pick up the knee-tapper and begin again. If he misses you, you get his chair and he has to start round the circle with the knee-tapper, looking for a new victim. It is a fast and furious game and you will all soon discover how vital it is to put the knee-tapper cleanly on to the centre chair, as going back to put it right can be disastrous!

Balloon Catching

Group size: 10 or more

Playing time: 10 minutes

Area: enough clear space for everybody to sit in a circle

You need: 2 blown-up balloons, a small piece of paper for everybody but the Thrower, numbered from 1 upwards

Sit in a circle and hand out the numbered bits of paper at random, leaving one person to be Thrower. The Thrower has the balloons and throws them up in the air, aiming to land them inside the circle, and calls out two numbers. The two people with those numbers instantly leap to their feet and dive for a balloon, catching it before it reaches the ground. If someone fails to catch a balloon before it reaches the ground, she loses a life; anybody losing three lives is out. The Thrower has ten throws and then changes places with someone in the circle.

This can be a very funny game, especially when both numbers dive for the same balloon!

Shoeing Horses

Group size: 10–20 (or more)

Playing time: 10–20 minutes

Area: clear space with a smooth or carpeted floor

You need: 2 light four-legged chairs with no sharp edges, 6 or 7 small plastic flowerpots or yoghurt pots, 2 blindfolds

Everybody sits in a circle. Put the two chairs facing each other at opposite ends of the circle. These are the horses. Choose two people to be Jockeys and sit one on each chair. Blindfold the Jockeys. Get everybody in the circle to make a noise, whispering, clapping, anything which covers the noise of you sneaking round the circle placing the flowerpots. Put the flowerpots upside-down at random round the inside of the circle. As soon as that is done, the noise stops and the Jockeys set off looking for the flowerpots. Hands and knees is

the best way for the Jockeys to get about. When a Jockey finds a flowerpot, he takes it back to his horse and slips it on to the base of one of its legs. He has to try and get flowerpots on to all four legs of his horse before the other Jockey does. He can only pick up one flowerpot at a time. He can pinch flowerpots (one at a time) from his opponent's horse, providing she is not touching her horse at the time. If a Jockey loses his sense of direction, which is easily done, and starts shoeing the wrong horse, that is his hard luck and he should be left alone to do it. Jockeys cannot fight, nor try to wrest a flowerpot away from the other Jockey. The horses must not be moved from their original positions.

A truly hilarious game, especially for the spectators!

All Change

Group size: 10–20 (or more)

Playing time: 10–20 minutes

Area: clear space

You need: chairs for all but 1 person

Arrange the chairs in a circle and get everybody sitting on them, then stand in the middle and say something like, 'All those wearing blue socks change places!' As soon as you have said that, everybody wearing blue socks must get up and move to another chair. They may not go back to their old chair. In the resulting confusion, you find a seat, which will leave one person in the middle with no chair to go to. That person now chooses something else to get people to change places. It can be anything – names, colour of eyes, whether they had a bath that morning – but clothes are often the easiest, since you can spot someone who is going to have to move and hover close by, ready to dive for her chair as soon as she leaves it.

Ladders

Group size: 10–20 (or more)

Playing time: 10 minutes

Area: clear space

Divide the group into two equal teams and get them to sit down facing each other, legs stretched out in front of them, feet just touching an opponent's feet. There should be roughly twenty to thirty centimetres between each person in a team. Number each person in the team from the top down to the bottom, so that the Ones from both teams have their feet touching, as do the Twos, the Threes and so on down the

lines. When this is done, you call a number. If, for example, you call 'Two', the Twos instantly leap to their feet and run down between the two teams, nimbly avoiding everybody's legs and only treading in the gaps between them until they reach the end. They then charge back up the line outside the teams to the top again, nimbly step over the Ones' legs and back into their own spaces. The first number Two back to his place wins a point for his team. You then call another number and another two opponents start their run down and up the human ladder. The team with the most points at the end wins.

Shopping

Group size: 10–20 (or more)

Playing time: 10–15 minutes

Area: large clear space without a slippery floor; carpet is ideal

You need: 4 prepared Shopkeepers' lists and 1 master list

Make up a list of twenty or so items, as sane or as zany as you like. Divide these items at random into four separate lists of equal length, numbering each list and marking on your master list which items appear on which Shopkeeper's list.

Choose four people to be Shopkeepers, give each of them a Shopkeeper's list and stand them on chairs, backs to the wall, in the four corners of the room. They are on chairs so that they are safe above the heads of the mob.

Call the rest of the group to you and tell them that you want them to find the shop that sells the first item on your master list – an elephant, for instance. The group instantly scatters round the four shopkeepers to ask whether they have an elephant to sell. The Shopkeepers can prevaricate a while, which is tantalizing, but must say Yes or No eventually.

When the Shopkeeper with an elephant for sale is found, the group form a long queue in front of his shop. The last person in the queue is out and must sit to one side. If you are playing with a large group, you can eliminate more than one each time, so that you are left with only a few Shoppers for the last few items.

Watch out for unscrupulous Shoppers barging into the queue and be absolutely ruthless about eliminating them; otherwise somebody might get a bit bruised.

The last Shopper left wins.

Locomotion

Group size: 20 or more

Playing time: 10–15 minutes

Area: large clear space

You need: a chair for all but 1 person

Choose someone to start; everybody else sits in a circle. The person in the middle decides on some method of getting about, like a train, a pogo-stick, swimming, flying – anything with a fairly definite action associated with it. He then goes round the inside of the circle, doing whatever he has chosen. For instance, if he has chosen to pogo, he would jump with two feet together round the circle. As he goes round the circle, he gently touches some people on the knee, who have to leave their chairs and form a line behind him, imitating his action. When he has got quite a few people behind him and he is near an empty chair, he shouts, 'All Change!' and everybody makes a dash for the remaining empty chairs. Since there is one chair too few, one person will be left in the middle of the circle to begin again with a new kind of locomotion.

Happy Families

Group size: 20 or more

Playing time: 10–15 minutes

Area: large clear space

You need: a pack of *Happy Families* cards or bits of paper divided into groups and marked like *Happy Families* cards

Give everybody one card each. When everybody has got a card, they start moving about the room, exchanging cards with as many people as they can until you shout 'Go!' As soon as they get this signal, they all look at the card in their hands and try to locate the rest of their family by shouting the family name as loudly as they can. The first family to get all its members together and sit down on the floor is the winner. When everybody has found their families, you can start the game again with the mixing-up process.

A *very* noisy game.

Menagerie

Group size: 20 or more

Playing time: 10–15 minutes

Area: large clear space

You need: small pieces of paper, divided into equal groups of about 4 or 5, with each group given the name of an animal

This game is virtually the same as *Happy Families*, except that, instead of shouting a family name, everybody must make their animal noise in order to find the other animals in the same group. So, a chicken will cluck, a tiger will roar and a mouse will squeak.

An *even noisier* game!

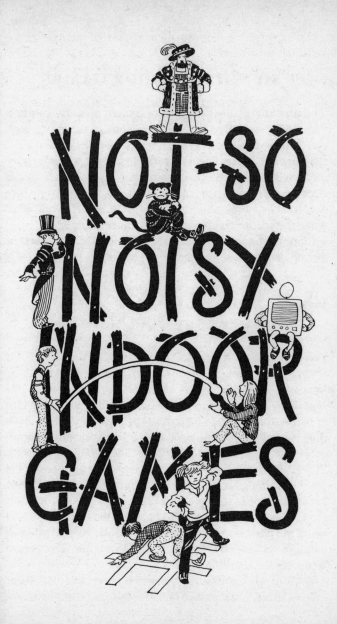

NOT-SO NOISY INDOOR GAMES

NOT SO NOISY INDOOR GAMES

The dividing line between noisy and not-so-noisy games is very fine, especially since the only game in the entire book that is impossible to play noisily is *King Silence*. However, the games in this section tend to be slightly quieter and rather more sedate than those in the last section. Often this is because they are largely spectator games and don't involve everybody rushing about at the same time. They are ideal when the space available indoors is rather limited.

Some of the word games can easily be played in the car or during long waits at stations or bus-stops.

Ghost

Group size: 2–6

Playing time: 5–15 minutes

Very simple. One person starts off with a letter of the alphabet – *G*, for example. The next person follows up with *H* perhaps, the next with a letter – such as *O*, and so on. Each time you say a letter you must have a possible word in mind; otherwise you are open to challenge. So, if you follow *G* with *Z*, you are almost certainly going to be challenged to say the word beginning *GZ* that you were thinking of. If you cannot produce a word, you lose a life. If you can produce a word, the Challenger loses a life. The object of the game is to avoid being the person who completes a word. If you find yourself *forced* to follow *GHOS* with *T*, you lose a life. The person who loses the fewest lives wins.

A word of warning: as the game progresses and letter follows letter, you may well find yourself in a position to force everybody to continue with one particular word, which is fine, providing you work out exactly where it is going to end and make sure that you don't land yourself with the last letter. Also, beware of words, like *hopeful*, whose first letters form shorter words; otherwise you might be caught unawares and forced to finish a word.

Human Noughts and Crosses

Group size: 2–8

Playing time: 3–5 minutes each go

Area: small clear floor space

You need: masking tape

Using the masking tape, mark out a large *Noughts and Crosses* grid on the floor, roughly one metre square.

The first two players then stand on opposite sides of the grid and take it in turns to place either a foot or a hand in a square. As in normal *Noughts and Crosses*, the idea is to get three squares in a row. However, since each player can only possess four squares at a time (two hands, two feet), there are bound to be times when a player has to leave a square to take over another, only to find that his opponent has taken possession of the square he has just left. To make things even more difficult, each player must keep his balance – if he falls over or any part of his body (apart from his hands and feet) touches the floor, he is out.

Potting

Group size: 2–8 (one at a time)

Playing time: 2 minutes each go

You need: 21 paper cups or yoghurt pots, stiff paper or card, Blu-tack, a table, a stop-watch or watch with a second hand

---

Number the bases of the cups from one to twenty-one. Draw round the top of a cup and cut out twenty-one card circles. Number these too. Stick the card circles at random on the table-top, fairly close together but not touching. Mix up the cups and place them in a stack in a clear space on the table.

The first person has just a minute and a half to try and put the numbered cups on top of the circles with the same numbers. When she has finished, the next person has a go. It is a fiendish game and far more difficult than it sounds. You can vary the time-limit to suit the age and skill of those playing.

Garibaldi

Group size: 2–8

Playing time: 10–30 minutes

Area: anywhere

One person begins by thinking of a famous person or character to be. He should choose someone he knows a fair bit about. Keeping quiet about exactly *who* he has thought of, he gives the rest of you the first letter of his character's name.

You all have to try and work out who the mystery person is – in two different ways.

First of all, supposing the letter you have been given is *G*, you can ask an *indirect question* by thinking of some famous person or character whose name also begins with *G*. You then ask the mystery person a question about *your* character like 'Are you Mickey Mouse's dog?' If the mystery person can guess who you are thinking of, he says, 'No, I am not Goofy.' You then have to think of some other character beginning with *G* to ask an indirect question about. However, if the mystery person hasn't a clue who *your* character is, you get a chance to ask a *direct question* about *his* character. You can have a stab at guessing who his character is, though it is probably more useful in the early stages to try and narrow the field a bit by finding out whether his character is male or female, dead or alive, real or fictional, when he lived, and so on. The mystery person can only answer Yes or No to a direct question. If, by chance, you hit on the mystery character in an indirect question, he has to own up: 'Yes, I am Garibaldi.' If you ask an indirect question and the mystery person doesn't think such a character exists, he can challenge you to name your character. If you are right, you get a direct question, but if you are wrong, you have to think of another indirect question.

For the first few times you play *Garibaldi*, it is worth insisting that nobody chooses characters that the rest haven't a reasonable chance of knowing about. Somebody who can trot out an endless series of Ancient Mycenaean Kings, for instance, is at an unfair advantage.

Poor Pussy

Group size: 4–10

Playing time: 5–10 minutes

Area: small clear space

A very silly game! Sit in a circle and choose someone to start as Pussy. Pussy gets down on his hands and knees and tries to make someone in the circle smile. He does this by miaowing, purring, rubbing up against his victim's legs – anything that a cat would do. The victim is only released from this barrage if he can say, 'Poor Pussy, poor Pussy' and pat Pussy on the head twice, all with a completely straight face. The slightest suspicion of a smile while he is doing this and he is done for. If he does smile, he has to give up his place to Pussy and become Pussy himself. Each Pussy is given three chances to charm somebody out of his chair and then another person is chosen to be Pussy. Failure is very rare as it is extremely difficult to resist Pussy when he wants your chair!

Smile Throwing

Group size: 4–12

Playing time: 5–10 minutes

Sit in a circle and choose someone to begin. She starts by smiling briefly, then covering her mouth with her hand, as though literally wiping the smile off her face. When she takes her hand away from her mouth, the smile has gone. She throws the smile in her hand to somebody else in the circle, who catches it, wipes it on to his face, smiles briefly and then wipes it off to throw at somebody else. Sounds loopy but great fun as you have to try and make everybody else laugh without getting the giggles yourself. Anybody caught with a glimmer of a smile on their lips out of turn is out. The last person left wins.

Henrietta

Group size: 4–10

Playing time: 5–15 minutes

You need: chairs for everyone

Have the chairs in an informal line. The person in the top chair – let's call her Henrietta – starts the game by calling the name of one of the other people and immediately starting to count rapidly from one to ten. The person she has named has to react instantly by calling somebody else's name and starting his own count from one to ten before Henrietta has finished hers. The person he has named has to call a name and start another count before his count is finished. And so on and so on, until somebody makes a slip. As soon as somebody fails to respond to his name before the count of ten is finished, he leaves his chair and goes down to the bottom chair, while everybody else who was below him in the line moves up a chair and fills up the gap he has left. Then the game starts again BUT this time things are different because the *chairs* keep the names of their original occupants and it is that name that the new occupants have to answer to. So, if Henrietta makes a mistake and has to go down to the bottom of the line, making everybody move up a chair, George, who has taken over Henrietta's chair, has to remember to respond to the name of Henrietta. If he or anybody else responds to their real name instead of the name of the chair, that is a mistake – and down to the bottom they go! The object of the game is to get to the top of the line and stay there – very difficult!

A fiendish added twist is to introduce an empty chair into the game, complete with its own name, which makes life much more difficult!

Fortunately, Unfortunately

Group size: 4–12

Playing time: 10–15 minutes

Sit in a circle. Choose somebody to start with a doom-laden statement like 'I'm sorry to have to tell you this, but we've been hit by a tornado.' Going clockwise round the circle, the person on her left follows this up with something beginning with *fortunately*. 'Fortunately, Air-Sea Rescue are on their way with a fleet of helicopters.' The next person on the left continues with something beginning with *unfortunately*. 'Unfortunately, somebody forgot to tell them where we are, so they had to return to base.' The next person begins with *fortunately*, the next with *unfortunately*, and so on round and round the circle until the weird and wonderful tale of mishap after mishap reduces everybody to fits of giggles. Give it a couple of goes to start with so that everybody gets the idea.

Guided Rockets

Group size: 4–20

Playing time: 5–15 minutes

Area: fair-sized clear space

You need: 2 blindfolds, 2 pieces of paper

Place the pieces of paper on the floor on opposite sides of your area. These represent two different planets. Choose two people to be Rockets aiming for the planets and blindfold them. Place each of the Rockets an equal distance away from their planets. Choose two more people, each of whom has a Rocket to guide by voice only. Taking it in turns, the Guiders can give an instruction to their Rockets. 'Four paces forwards,' 'Turn through ninety degrees,' 'One step to your left,' 'Two small steps to your right,' and so on. They cannot give composite instructions like 'One small step to your left and two forward.' The idea is for each Guider to try and get his Rocket to its planet before his opponent gets her Rocket to the other planet. There is no going back, so if a Rocket misunderstands an instruction, the Guider is stuck with it. The first Rocket with both its feet on its planet has won and four more people can have a go.

You can add to the difficulty of this game by choosing people to stand between Rockets and planets as obstacles the Rockets have to get past. If a Rocket hits either an obstacle or the other Rocket, it is exploded and has lost.

Picture Pieces

Group size: 4–20 (or more)

Playing time: 5–15 minutes

You need: at least 1 full-colour picture from a magazine for each person, Blu-tack

Cut each picture into five pieces. Keep one and stick the remaining four pieces of each picture at random round the walls.

Give each person one of the reserved pieces and tell them to go and find the other four bits, which isn't as easy as it sounds. You can play this game in two ways:

1) The first person with a complete picture correctly fitted together wins.

2) As people complete their picture, give them another piece. The person with the greatest number of complete pictures when you blow a whistle wins. You will need to cut up a lot more pictures than you have players.

Shooting Fish

Group size: 4–20 (or more)
Playing time: 3–5 minutes

Everybody except you sits down. Bend your left arm and hold it horizontally in front of your body. You are marking the surface of a river or sea. Use your other hand to be a fish swimming below the surface of the water. Every so often, your fish leaps out of the water and rises above the level of your other arm. Then, and only then, may the group try to shoot it by clapping their hands together once. Keep your fish moving fast and they'll miss most of the time, especially if you fool them by pretending to bring your fish out and having it turn just below the surface of the water.

On the last go, the group has only one shot between the lot of them, so if one person shoots when the fish is still in the water, you've won and they've lost. You'll win this game more often than not!

Continuous Mime

Group size: 4–20 (or more)

Playing time: 15–20 minutes

Area: a room with a door

Choose three people to go outside. The rest of you choose something zany for them to mime – playing tennis, wallpapering, robbing a bank – anything that is short and fairly easily mimed. Call the first person in and tell him what you have chosen. Give him a moment to think and then call the second person in. The first person then has to mime the thing you have chosen to the second person. When he has finished, he sits down and it is the second person's turn. She has to mime what she *thinks* she saw to the third person when he is called in. He then has to try to and guess what he is being shown. Give him three guesses and then tell him. Choose three more people to go out and start again.

King Silence

Group size: 4–20 (or more)

Playing time: 10–15 minutes

Area: clear space

'I am the King of Silence and you will be summoned one by one to my court!' Seated in the centre of a room with the rest of the group in a circle on the floor round you, your face solemn, your voice grave, explain how to play the game. Very simply, you point an imperious finger at one person and he has to get up from where he is sitting and make his way across to you and sit down by your side. It is not as easy as it sounds because he must make the move in *absolute* silence. If a shoe squeaks, a knee cracks or a floorboard creaks, he has lost and must return to his place. Everybody else must stay silent too, of course, so that you can pick up the slightest sound. The first three people to sit down silently beside you have won.

Earth, Air, Water

Group size: 5–20 (or more)

Playing time: 10–15 minutes

Area: clear space

You need: a small ball or tennis ball

All sit in a circle and choose someone to be the Caller. The Caller stands inside the circle, ball in hand. She then gently throws the ball to someone in the circle, saying at the same time 'Earth', 'Air' or 'Water' and starting to count steadily from one to five. The person she has thrown the ball to catches it and must throw the ball back to her before the count gets to five, at the same time naming a creature that normally lives in the element she mentioned. Easy, you might think. Not a bit of it! The people in the circle are not allowed to name a creature more than once and so rapidly run out of the obvious creatures like *tiger* for Earth, *sardine* for Water and *swallow* for Air. Then the fun starts, as they desperately try to think of a creature that hasn't been used before under the pressure of the count to five. If they name a creature that has been used before or fail to name something correctly by the time five is reached, they are out. Vague words like 'fish', 'insect' or 'mammal' are not allowed.

Killer

Group size: 5–20

Playing time: 5 minutes each go

Area: clear space

You need: a small piece of paper for each player, a hat or bowl

---

Mark one of the pieces of paper with a cross and fold it over. Fold the other pieces of paper the same way and put them all in the hat.

Shake the hat so that the pieces of paper are thoroughly mixed up and pass the hat round so that everybody can take one. Everybody surreptitiously opens their piece of paper, making sure that nobody else can see what is on it. It is very important, if difficult, to keep a straight face at this point. The person with the marked paper is the Killer and sets about silently murdering as many people as he can by winking at them. If you spot that you are being winked at, you instantly die as dramatically as you like and cannot tell the others who the Killer is. The idea is for the Killer to try and bump everybody off before any of them spot who he is. It is therefore very important for the Killer to be a sly winker, killing people with just a flicker of an eyelid. Killers who have to screw up the whole of one side of their face to slay someone are unlikely to get away with it for long. As soon as the Killer is spotted or has managed to bump everybody off, collect up all the bits of paper, fold them up again and put them back in the hat for another go.

Pip, Pop

Group size: 5–20 (or more)

Playing time: 5–10 minutes

Couldn't be simpler. You point at someone and say PIP. He has to reply instantly with POP. You say POP, he says PIP. You say PIP POP, he says POP PIP, and vice versa. You say PIP PIP POP, he must reply POP POP PIP, and so on. When you POP, the person you point to must PIP. When you PIP, he must POP. If anybody gets it wrong or fluffs it, he is out. If you jump from person to person, you'll keep them on their toes. You can increase the complexity of your PIPs and POPs as you whittle the group down, though make sure that *you* remember which combination you have used.

Stand Up, Sit Down

Group size: 5–20 (or more)

Playing time: 3 minutes

Area: almost anywhere

Very simple, and ideal for starting a party. Get everybody sitting down, either on chairs or on the floor, while you remain standing. Tell them that you've noticed a very peculiar thing recently – whenever you stand up, everybody sits down and whenever you sit down, everybody leaps to their feet; as you say this, you sit down and, with a bit of luck, they will all stand up. They may need a bit of prompting the first time, but they'll soon catch on. Stand up and sit down a few more times – try to catch them out by pretending to sit down – until you have got them going up and down like yo-yos. Then introduce the next element. You have also noticed that whenever you have your arms up in the air, everybody has their arms down by their sides, and vice versa. Try this a couple of times and then combine the up and down arms with the standing up and sitting down for guaranteed instant confusion!

A What?

Group size: 8–14

Playing time: 5–10 minutes

Area: small clear space

Sit in a close circle. One person starts the game by pretending to hand something to her left-hand neighbour, saying at the same time what it is. 'This is a hippopotamus,' she says, for instance. Her left-hand neighbour, naturally astounded at being handed a hippopotamus, says, 'A what?' back to her and she repeats, 'A hippopotamus.' Her left-hand neighbour then hands the hippopotamus to his left-hand neighbour, saying, 'This is a hippopotamus.' The neighbour says, 'A what?' but by this time the person who gave the hippo to him has forgotten what it was and has to turn back to the first person to ask, 'A what?' The first person answers again 'A hippopotamus,' her neighbour turns back to his neighbour and says, 'A hippopotamus.' His neighbour then turns to *her* left-hand neighbour, hands him the hippo and the whole thing begins again with 'A what?' coming back around the circle to the first person each time and the answer being sent back from person to person to where the hippo is. Try this for a while so that everybody gets the idea; the first person then starts off something going the other way. Pretending to hand something to her right-hand neighbour, she says, 'This is a giraffe.' 'A what?' says her neighbour in some surprise, and so on, just like the hippo. The fun really starts when the hippo and the giraffe meet round the other side of the circle and the people there have to cope with the mind-boggling confusion of two lots of 'A what?' coming at them from different directions.

Don't just stick to hippos and giraffes – do your worst!

Electric Circuits

Group size: 8–15

Playing time: 5–10 minutes

Area: clear floor space in a room with a door

Send one person out of the room. The rest of you sit in a tight circle, holding hands with your neighbours and making sure that your hands are hidden behind your backs. Quietly choose somebody to be the Generator. The Generator sends a current round the circle by gently squeezing one of his neighbours' hands. His neighbour then gently squeezes her other neighbour's hand and so on round the circle, until the current gets back to the Generator. The Generator then sends the current back round the circle in the opposite direction.

Each time the current reaches the Generator, he sends it back the way it has come.

Choose a few people round the circle to be pieces of electrical equipment like televisions, radios, mixers, alarms – anything that makes a recognizable noise. These people stay quiet until the electric current from the Generator reaches them, when they are switched on. They make their noise and then pass the current on round the circle. Each time the current reaches them, from either side, their noise is triggered off.

Call the person outside back in again, stand him in the middle of the circle and start the current going. He has to try and work out exactly who the Generator is – which is surprisingly difficult. Give him three guesses and then send somebody else outside, choose another Generator and different bits of electrical equipment and start again.

The Name Game

Group size: 8–20

Playing time: 5–10 minutes

Area: clear space

Stand in a fairly close circle, facing inward, not touching shoulders but without large gaps between people. Choose someone to begin. He calls the name of somebody else in the circle and immediately starts walking towards her across the circle. She must call another person's name and start walking towards him before the first person has reached her. And so on. Anybody fluffing or making a mistake loses a life – and you only have three to lose! The game requires some concentration, especially for small groups – when the circle is also small – but it is great fun and an ideal way of getting to know everybody's name.

Rabbits

Group size: 10–20 (or more)

Playing time: 10–15 minutes

Area: clear space

Get everybody standing up in a circle around you. You are a big bad farmer with a big bad gun and you *hate* rabbits. They are the rabbits. Point your finger, gun-like, at a rabbit and say BANG! The rabbit's only defence against this assault is to put both her hands up to her ears and to waggle them as though they were rabbit's ears. She must do this the moment you shoot her or she is dead and must sit down. Try this for a while round the circle until everybody has got the idea. Easy, they think. Not a bit of it. You now bring out your biggest

baddest gun, which has a much wider spread than your old one. Now, when you shoot a rabbit, you are also shooting at the rabbits on either side. The rabbit you actually point at uses the old defence and waggles his ears, but the rabbits either side of him only have to waggle the ear *nearest* to the rabbit that was shot at. So the rabbit to the right of your intended victim has to waggle her *left* ear and the rabbit to the left must waggle his *right* ear. Any rabbit caught waggling the wrong number of ears at any time is dead, as is any rabbit that doesn't waggle the right number of ears quick enough.

And now the game gets really fiendish. Rabbits will make mistakes and die, leaving gaps in the circle. Where this happens, the rabbits must ignore the gaps and treat the rabbit on the other side of the gap as a new neighbour. So, they must keep a careful eye on what is happening, not only to themselves and their immediate neighbours but also to newly created neighbours as old neighbours come to a sticky end. Rabbits who allow their attention to wander are soon dead rabbits.

Moving Marbles

Group size: 10–20

Playing time: 5–10 minutes

Area: clear space

You need: 2 bowls (1 empty, 1 full of marbles), for each team, chairs or a bench for each team

Divide the group into two equal teams, who sit in two lines facing each other. Each team has an empty and a full bowl at the top of the line. On the word 'Go!' the first person in each team takes one marble out of the full bowl and passes it to her neighbour, who passes it to his neighbour, and so on down the line until the marble reaches the end of the team. As soon as the marble gets to the end of the team, it starts being passed hand to hand back up the team behind the team's backs and into the empty bowl at the top.

As soon as the first person passes the first marble to her neighbour, she reaches back into the full bowl for another marble to pass down the team, and so on, until there is a continuous stream of marbles passing down the front of and back up behind each team. The first team with all its marbles moved from one bowl to the other wins, so the marbles must move fast and everybody has to keep their wits about them. A dropped marble stops the passage of the rest until it has been retrieved and may lose valuable seconds.

Who Has the Ball?

Group size: 10–20 (or more)

Playing time: 10–15 minutes

Area: clear space in a room with a door

You need: a tennis ball, a medium-sized ball, a football

Choose one person to go out, while the rest of you sit in a circle. As soon as he is outside, take the tennis ball and roll it gently across the circle. As soon as it reaches somebody, she must nudge it on across the circle to somebody else. The ball must be kept gently rolling the whole time and must not be held. The person outside must give three warning knocks, all together, spaced out or in any combination he feels like, before coming back into the room. As soon as the third knock is heard, whoever has the ball must immediately try to hide it somewhere about her person, while everybody else also pretends to be hiding the ball. She has got to be quick about it as the person will burst through the door as soon as he has given the third knock and may see her with the ball. He has three quick guesses at who has the ball and then the person hiding the ball goes out.

Play the game with the tennis ball for a couple of goes until everybody has got the idea and then gradually introduce the larger balls, which are very difficult to hide successfully!

Zig-zag

Group size: 10 or more

Playing time: 5–10 minutes

Area: clear space

You need: 2 balloons

Divide into two equal groups and stand in two lines facing each other. Number each line from one upwards. Team A is all the odd-numbered people in one row and all the even-numbered people in the other. Team B is all the other people.

Give a balloon to the first person in each row, who, on the word 'Go!', throws the balloon across to her team-mate, number two in the opposite row. Number two then throws it back across to number three and so on down the line. You must not leave your place to catch the balloon. The first team to get its balloon to the end of the line wins. This isn't as simple as it sounds since the two balloons are criss-crossing the lines the whole time and a dropped balloon must go right back to the top of the line.

Cops and Robbers

Group size: 10–20 (or more)

Playing time: 10–15 minutes

Area: large clear space

You need: 3 or 4 blindfolds

Choose a Robber (ideally someone prepared to be energetic, wearing plimsolls or something similar) and tie her feet together with one of the blindfolds, so that she can move about only by jumping with two feet together. Choose two Cops and blindfold them. The Cops have to try and catch the Robber as she moves about inside the circle which all the other players form around them. At any time and as often as they like, the Cops can call out, 'Where are you, Robber?' and the Robber must immediately stop moving long enough to clap her hands loudly twice. Gradually the Cops get cleverer about pinpointing where the noise is coming from and the Robber gets tired, making it easier for the Cops to catch her. Sometimes, however, the Robber is extra-agile and keeps evading the Cops by the skin of her teeth, in which case you can either declare her the winner and let different people have a go, or call up reinforcements and create an extra Cop to help out.

Pity the Blind

Group size: 12 or more

Playing time: 10–15 minutes

Area: clear space

You need: blindfolds for half the group, a stop-watch or something similar

Choose one person to be Watch-keeper and divide the rest of the group into two, one half to be the Blind, the other half to be the Creepers. Stand the Blind in a circle, close enough to be able to touch each other's outstretched hands, and blindfold them. Put the first two Creepers into the circle and give them just a minute to get out of the circle without being touched by the Blind, which requires cunning and stealth. The Blind may not move their feet but only have to touch a Creeper to make a catch. Any Creeper who gets out in under a minute wins a point for his side. As soon as all the Creepers have had a go, the Creepers change places with the Blind. The side with the most points at the end wins.

Leader of the Orchestra

Group size: 15 or more

Playing time: 10 minutes

Area: clear space in a room with a door

Choose someone to go out while the rest of you sit in a circle. As soon as she's outside the door, choose someone sitting in the circle to be Leader of the Orchestra, who starts miming an instrument, like the violin, harp, drums, flute, bongoes, gong – anything. Everybody else must copy his actions. Every so often, the Leader changes the instrument he is playing and everybody else follows suit. As soon as the Orchestra has got the hang of this, call the person outside back in again. She has got to try and spot who is the Leader and has three quick guesses. The trick is not to stare at the Leader, waiting for his next change, as that's a dead give-away. If she guesses right, or if she's completely fooled and gets it wrong three times, the Leader goes out, you choose a new Leader and the game starts again.

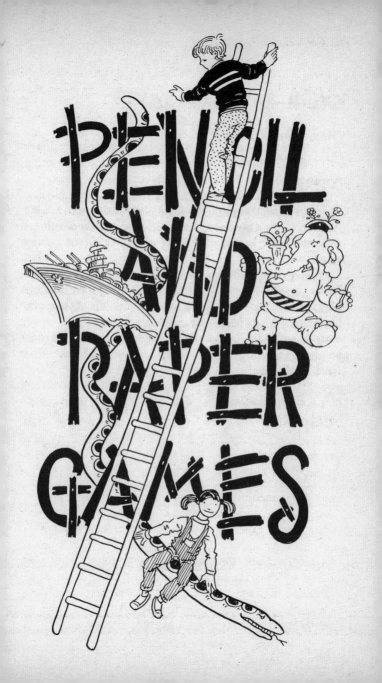

PENCIL AND PAPER GAMES

PENCIL AND PAPER GAMES

Pencil and paper games usually provide a much needed breather from the feverish excitement of games like *Lurky* and *Fishtails*. However, there is nothing to stop them being as noisy and funny as the most energetic of outdoor games.

Organization is all important in pencil and paper games – especially since there may be time to kill between collecting papers in and giving them out again, as in *Big Battleships*. A game of *Smile Throwing* to fill the gap stops people getting bored.

Be careful not to allow too long for 'thinking' in games like *Poetry Consequences* or you'll end up with people waiting hours for inspiration to hit them. A time limit of, say, two minutes is a good idea and keeps things moving.

Make sure that everybody has something comfortable to sit on, something to lean on, plenty of paper, rubbers and a pencil sharpener.

Feely Box

Group size: 2–10

Playing time: 5 minutes

You need: a medium-sized cardboard box, 6 polythene bags, sellotape, 6 objects with interesting textures, a sharp knife, a piece of paper and a pencil for everybody

Carefully cut six openings at even intervals round the sides of the box by drawing circles roughly ten centimetres in diameter and making six evenly spaced cuts from the centre of each circle out to the circumference. You then have an opening big enough for a hand, but the flaps make it difficult to see inside. Sellotape the open end of a polythene bag over the inside of each of the openings you have made, making sure that the bags are firmly attached. Seal up the top of the box (and the bottom, if necessary) and decorate the outside if you want to. Put one object into each opening.

Everyone has to put a hand into each opening in turn, have a feel and then write down what they think they have just felt. They must not peek in through the opening, nor try to take the object out. The person with the most correct answers wins.

Here are some suggestions for feely objects: cold spaghetti; sandpaper; paperclips; marbles; silk; a grape; a deflated balloon.

Smelly Boxes

Group size: 2–10

Playing time: 5 minutes

You need: 6 small boxes or yoghurt pots, sellotape, 6 objects with a distinctive smell, a piece of paper and a pencil for everybody

Put one smelly object into each box and cover the top with a piece of paper punctured with a few holes, tightly stuck down with sellotape. Number each box.

The game is then very simple. Everybody has to try and guess the smells and write them down. The person with the most correct answers is the winner.

Here are some suggestions for smelly objects: lemon; chocolate; cinnamon; coffee; dirty sock; bacon; cheese; curry powder; peach; tea; soap.

Giant Snakes and Ladders

Group size: 2–20

Playing time: 10–15 minutes

You need: a *Snakes and Ladders* board (you probably won't want to write out masses of instructions, so draw up a board with only 49 squares), a die or some dice, a counter for everybody, paper for instructions, Blu-tack, pencil and paper for everybody

Think up enough simple instructions for there to be one for each square on the board, excluding the squares at the bottom of ladders, those at the tops of snakes and the last square. The instructions can be very simple, such as 'Count up to 100 as fast as you can', 'Take ten steps backwards' and 'Write down your favourite joke.' Number each instruction and stick them up at random round the room – or round the house, if you feel like giving the game more scope.

Taking it in turns, each member of the group throws a die and moves his counter along the board for the same number of squares as he has thrown. He then has to go and find the instruction with the same number as the square he has landed on. He must do what the instruction says before he can come back to the board and have another throw.

As with normal *Snakes and Ladders*, anybody landing at the foot of a ladder moves up it and looks for the number at the top of the ladder, while anybody landing on the head of the snake slithers down it and looks for the number where the tail stops. The first person to the last square on the board wins.

Cook Up a Story

Group size: 3–10

Playing time: 5 minutes

Area: anywhere comfortable to sit down

You need: pencil and paper for each player, a stop-watch or watch

Think up a list of ten totally unrelated objects – a daisy, an elephant, a teaspoon, the Eiffel Tower, a banana split, and so on.

Sit everybody down, read them the list and then stick it up somewhere everybody can see it easily. On the word 'Go!' everybody has three minutes in which to try to write a story including *all* the objects on your list, trying also to get their stories to make sense (of a sort). When the time is up, these literary masterpieces are read out and a vote is taken for the best.

Blindfold Drawing

Group size: 3–10

Playing time: 10 minutes

You need: a blindfold, a pad of paper, something to draw with

Blindfold one person and give her the pencil and pad of paper. Ask her to try and draw something, like an elephant, a castle or a ladder. You'll be amazed how difficult this is, especially if you are under the blindfold, and how funny it is to watch as the blindfold artist carefully draws the elephant's ear half-way up one of its back legs! When one person has finished, another person has a go – until you are bored with it.

The Dictionary Game

Group size: 3–20 (or more)

Playing time: 20–40 minutes

You need: a big dictionary, pencils and a supply of paper for everybody, Blu-tack

Go through the dictionary picking out a number of unusual words. You will probably need three words and definitions for each player (or team). Write each player's words with their definitions on a piece of paper to give to him, making a note for yourself of which player has which words. Then write out each word clearly on a large sheet of paper, ready to stick up on the wall.

Give each player his list of words and definitions. They then have five minutes in which to make up two false definitions for each word on their lists, making sure that none of the other players can see what they are doing. They should write all three definitions for each word (one true and two false) on another sheet of paper so that there is no way that the opposition can see which definition is the true one.

When the five minutes is up, the players take it in turn to read out words with their three definitions. Stick the word that is being read out up on the wall so that everybody can see how it is spelt. As soon as all three definitions have been read out, all the other players quietly decide which definition each of them thinks is the true definition and write it down on a piece of paper. After a couple of minutes, all the bits of paper are collected up, the true definition is read out and everybody who guessed correctly is given a point.

The game continues until all the words have been read out; the player with the highest number of points wins.

If you are playing with more than five people, you should divide the group into equal teams, giving each team a list of words and definitions; otherwise the game can become very lengthy. You can either play it that the team has to decide collectively which is a correct definition, or you can give each person in the team a vote; correct votes score points for the team. If you play this last way, it is absolutely essential that you have equal numbers in the teams; otherwise the larger teams have an advantage over the smaller ones. Alternatively, you could try to work out some way of handicapping the larger teams, but this can get rather complicated.

A baffling and frustrating game that is tremendous fun to play.

Adverts

Group size: 3–15

Playing time: 5–10 minutes

You need: 6 full-page advertisements from magazines, each for a single product and without a lot of lettering (ideally, the brand name should be at the bottom or top of the advert, so that it can be cut off easily), 6 sheets of paper, slightly bigger than the advertisements, scissors and glue, pencil and paper for everyone

Carefully cut round the outline of the product being advertised, leaving a hole the same shape. Cut off the brand names. Stick each advert on to a sheet of paper, number them and stick them up round the room.

Everybody then has to try and guess what the advert is for, which is sometimes more difficult than it sounds, especially with bottle or box silhouettes. The person with the most correct answers at the end wins.

Big Battleships

Group size: 3–20 (or more)

Playing time: 20–40 minutes (or more)

You need: a sheet of paper and a pencil for each player or team, a large sheet of paper, a different coloured pencil for each player or team

Mark out a grid of fifteen by fifteen squares on each player's (or team's) sheet of paper. Mark out a similar grid with bigger squares on your large sheet of paper. This is your master grid. Number the grids along the top from one to fifteen and letter them down the side from *A* to *O*, so that each square has a reference – A3, M15 and so on.

Give each player (or team) a grid, which represents the sea, and tell him to mark his navy secretly on to it by shading in the relevant number of squares. Each navy consists of one battleship, two cruisers, two frigates and three submarines. The symbols for these are as follows:

Battleship

Cruiser

Frigate

Submarine

If you're playing with four players or less, it's worth reducing the grid to ten by ten squares and giving the players more vessels so that they have a good chance of hitting something when they fire.

When each player has finished placing his navy, ask him to write his name at the top of the paper and gather the grids in, making sure that nobody sees a grid that isn't theirs. Mark each person's navy on to your master grid, using a different colour for each team. It doesn't matter if it turns out that more than one ship is occupying a square on your master grid. This process takes some time, so it is well worth planning to have something else that everybody can get on with while you are marking out the master grid. Send them all off for tea or have another game going that they can play without your help, such as *Garibaldi*. You will need a good ten to fifteen minutes at this point. When the master grid is ready, the game can start.

Give each player his grid back. Taking it in turns, each player fires a salvo of three shots into the sea by naming three squares – for example, 'A3, M15, L4.' He should mark on his grid exactly which squares he has fired into for future reference. You, on the master grid, also mark which squares have been fired into. When the salvo has been fired, you tell the firer whether he has hit anything in those squares. If he has hit something, you give him the square's reference and tell him he has made a hit but do not tell him what he has hit or who it belongs to. The only exception to this is when somebody's ship has been hit on all its squares, when you tell the person who scored the final hit that she has sunk a ship, what she has hit and who it belonged to. A player may not fire into a square occupied by one of his own ships – or, if he does, he scores a hit on his own ship. It is well worth everybody making some small mark in each square that has been fired at so that shots are not wasted by firing into squares that have already been hit.

The idea of the game is to bomb everybody else's navy out of the water before they manage to do the same to you. As soon as somebody's entire navy has been sunk, they drop out of the game. The last person left with a ship or part of a ship still intact wins.

If you are playing with more than about five people, you should divide up into teams and give everybody in the team turns at firing the salvoes.

Poetry Consequences

Group size: 4–10

Playing time: 10–20 minutes

Area: somewhere comfortable to sit

You need: a pencil and a sheet of paper for each player

If the idea of poetry fills you with gloom, don't let it. No self-respecting poet would be seen anywhere near this game! It's ideal for *bad* poets; the worse your poetry is, the better the game is!

Everybody thinks of a suitable title for a poem – *To an Elephant's Knees* or *I Wish I Were a Bumble Bee* might be possibilities for this game. Write your title at the top of the paper and keep quiet about it. Now write the first two lines of a poem underneath the title. Make it like a ballad, in the same metre as *Casabianca* by Felicia Hemans:

> The boy stood on the burning deck
> Whence all but he had fled.

So, if you are writing the Bumble Bee poem, your first two lines could be:

> 'I wish I were a bumble bee,'
> The donkey sadly said.

Now fold the top of your paper over, so that it covers the title but leaves your first two lines visible, and pass it on to the person on your left. He then has to think of two more lines to finish off your first verse, remembering that the last line of the verse should rhyme roughly with the second line. So suppose he adds on:

> 'Flitting about across wide fields,
> White clouds above my head.'

He then folds over the top of the paper to cover up the whole of the first verse and writes two lines of a second verse before handing it on to his left hand neighbour. As the poems progress round the circle, their story lines go off in all sorts of wonderful directions since, after the first verse is completed, nobody has the faintest idea how any of the poems started off, nor which poem they happen to be adding to at that moment.

After about six verses, call a halt. The last person finishes off a verse and then writes a sane or silly consequence, such as:

> That'll teach them not to fry eggs in aeroplanes!

The poems are then all rolled up completely and mixed up. Everybody takes a poem, unrolls it and reads out their epic – and the hilarious poetic twists and contortions are revealed!

Nobody need feel worried about writing this kind of poetry, where the rules are very lax. Rhymes and line lengths can be very loose (they often have to be) and providing nobody ends a line with 'wasp', which is impossible to find a rhyme for, *Poetry Consequences* can be the greatest fun – even for confirmed poetry-haters!

Drawing Clumps

Group size: 6–20 (or more)

Playing time: 15–20 minutes

You need: a pencil and some sheets of paper for each group

Write down a list of about twenty objects for the players to draw. Keep them fairly simple, like an orange, a giraffe, a pond, and so on.

Divide your group into pairs or small groups. Call one person from each group up to you and whisper the first item on your list to them. It is very important that the other people in the groups should not hear what you are saying. They then go back to their groups and try to draw the object you have given them, while the other members in the group try to guess what it is. The person who is drawing is not allowed to speak; she can only shake or nod her head to help the guessers along. When the group have guessed correctly, the next person from that group comes back to you and must whisper the first item to you before you will give him the next thing on your list. He then goes back to the group and draws this new object for the group to guess. The first group to guess the last item on your list is the winner. It is well worth pointing out before you start that if the guessers get so excited that they shout the answers, the other groups will hear and they will have given the game away.

TREASURE HUNTS

TREASURE HUNTS

A treasure hunt is a game in which something has been hidden and has to be found by following a series of clues. They are ideally suited to outdoors, especially if you have woods or a park you can use, though you can also have indoor hunts on a small scale. Treasure hunts can be very simple or really complicated, depending on how long you want them to run and how much time you have to prepare them. It is worth spending some time preparing a hunt carefully so that it will work well. Ideally, all the hunters should start off at the same time and get to the end of the trail at roughly the same time, so that nobody has to hang about for long at the end.

If you are planning a treasure hunt for the first time, it is a good idea to have a rehearsal by trying your clues or trails on some unsuspecting person who isn't going to be involved in the hunt. You can then get some idea of how long the hunt will take and if there are any unforeseen snags, like misleading clues, that haven't occurred to you.

There are a number of ideas for treasure hunts in this section, all of which are adaptable to your needs – the area you have, the time you have and the number of hunters playing. If you want to get *really* complicated, you can even combine different types of treasure hunt.

Remember that if you are laying trails in a public park you should collect up all the pieces and any other litter before you leave.

Simple Trail

Group size: 2–20 (or more)

Playing time: 15–45 minutes

Area: woods and scrubland, a garden or a large house – almost anywhere except wide open space.

You need: several small, coloured bits of paper or material (one colour or pattern for each hunter or team), drawing pins (for trees) or Blu-tack (for walls), a treasure for each trail

Lay your trails, making sure that none of the hunters see you doing it. Make sure that the first piece of each trail is clearly visible from your starting point. After that, make sure that each piece you pin up in a trail is visible for a hunter standing by the previous piece. Make the trails of equal length, using the same number of pieces for each; it doesn't matter how devious and twisted they are. Use the last piece to mark the treasure at the end of each trail. Make sure that all the treasures are some way from each other as you don't want any hunter to stumble across the wrong treasure.

Give each hunter (or team of hunters) a piece of their trail paper so that they all know what they are following. As soon as they are told to 'Go!', the hunters set off to follow their own trail; the first one back with the right treasure wins.

Additional ideas

1) Each piece of paper in each trail could have a letter on it, which, when collected together in sequence, spell a word that the hunter has to give before she gets her treasure.

2) You could also combine that idea with the *Scavenger Hunt* (page 18) and make the hunter scavenge something

beginning with the letter on the trail paper before moving on to the next one.

3) Give each hunter a pencil and paper and have a task or puzzle written on each trail paper that the hunter has to solve or do before moving on. These problems can be very simple or very silly – 'Stand on one leg and count to 100'; 'Draw an elephant'; '4 × 32 = ?'; 'Where is the Eiffel Tower?'; and so on.

Simple Circular Hunt

Group size: 4–20 (or more)

Playing time: 30–45 minutes

Area: woods, garden, playground, park, house – anywhere with plenty of identifiable landmarks or distinctive features.

You need: 6–10 empty tins (or, jars, yoghurt pots, small boxes or something similar), at least the same number of hiding-places, enough small bits of paper to have one in each hiding-place for each hunter or team of hunters, a treasure for each hunter or team

Choose your hiding-places and think up a clue for each one to help the hunters find it. The clues can be as difficult and as devious as you like, or fairly obvious, depending on the age and ingenuity of your hunters. Mysterious clues will take some time to work out and so the hunt will go on longer. It *is* important that the hiding-places should not be too close together, so that one hunter does not spot another at the next place, making it unnecessary for him to unravel his clue. Make as many copies of each clue as you have hunters or teams.

Think of your hiding-places as a circle and work out the order in which you want them to be found. Place the clues for each hiding-place in a tin at the hiding-place before, so that the clues for the blasted oak are hidden by the old sundial and the clues for the old sundial are hidden by the cattle-grid and so on in a continuous chain. Mark each of the treasures with a hunter's name and place each one in one of the hiding-place tins at even intervals round the circle. When you put a treasure into a tin, remember to remove one of the clues and put the same name on it.

Give each of the hunters the clue with his name on it, which will start him off looking for the hiding-place *after* the place where his treasure lies. When a hunter finds his first hiding-place, he takes a clue out of the tin and starts looking for the next place. If he finds a treasure in the tin with somebody else's name on it, he must leave it there and not tell anybody where it is. Eventually, a hunter will work round the circle of hiding-places until he gets to the tin with his treasure in it. The first hunter to do so wins.

Since this hunt is also a race of sorts, it is well worth the hunters being a bit cunning once they have worked out a clue and trying to get to a hiding-place without letting on to any of the other hunters where it is. Otherwise, the other hunters might well catch up too soon and win.

Additional ideas for clues

1) Simple codes. a) Number each letter of the alphabet from one to twenty-six and use numbers instead of letters to write your clues. b) Use mirror writing. Write down your clues by watching your hand and pencil in the mirror. Or (much easier), place a piece of carbon paper with the black carbon facing upwards on a table and lay two pieces of paper on top of it. Write your clues firmly on the top piece of paper with a biro and the clue will come out backwards on the underside of the second sheet of paper. You could put the paper and carbon into a typewriter like that too. c) Add to the confusion by writing your coded or reversed message in groups of four letters or numbers.

2) Riddles. They don't have to be brilliant, just a bit confusing and time-consuming to work out. For instance, the cattle grid could be:

> Two feet may pass but four are bound:
> This cage's bars lie on the ground.

Baddies

Of course, treasure hunts can be great fun, skulking in and out of trees, deciphering cryptic clues, fully aware that the next hunter is catching up fast, setting trails off in the wrong direction as red herrings to confuse the rest. However, in all these hunts you are pitting your tracking and detecting skills against your friends, who you know and like. Imagine then what it would be like to have a real baddie to play against. Picture yourself beating The Galactic Dictator to a vital star map that will save the universe; sneaking off with Robin Hood to rescue King Richard from the Sheriff of Nottingham's evil clutches; joining forces with the wizard Gandalf to thwart the dark power of Mordor.

Introducing a baddie into a treasure hunt can be quite simple and doesn't take much more time to organize than a conventional hunt. You need a willing outsider to be the baddie and another person to represent the forces opposed to the baddie and explain what the hunt is about. This sort of hunt works best if both the baddie and the good guy keep out of sight, and don't let on what is going to happen before the hunt starts.

Suppose you decide that the hunt is going to try and prevent The Galactic Dictator getting his evil hands on that star map by getting to it first. To prepare this, you would need to draw a rough star map on a large sheet of paper and cut it up into the same number of pieces as there are hunters. Then follow the instructions for the *Simple Trail*, using pieces of the map instead of treasure.

The Dictator and the good guy will need some kind of simple costume or disguise. The Dictator could use black rubbish sacks, black gloves and a black mask, which, combined with an arrogant attitude and some heavy breathing as he speaks, conjure up a super-villain. The good guy, a shy boffin from a highly secret research establishment, only needs a white coat, spectacles and a nervously intellectual manner.

Gather everybody together so that the Boffin can explain that he has just discovered that the vital star map was fragmented by accident when a patrol ship crashed on this planet. To make matters worse, the Dictator has discovered some fiendish way of detecting the presence of the pieces of map and is even now tracking them down. (The Dictator is seen lurking evilly round a corner, hissing.) Luckily, the

Boffin happens to have with him some puzzling pieces of paper that he thinks might have some use in helping the hunters find the bits of map. (He hands out the first clues.) But beware, he warns; should the Dictator actually catch a hunter, he will be able to use his dark powers to enslave the miserable hunter for the period of one minute, during which time the slave cannot move. Of course, the Dictator, being *such* an evil person, is quite capable of trying to extract information from his hapless prisoner by fair means or, more probably, foul. So it is important that the hunters should evade the Dictator and be doubly careful not to lead him to any of the hiding-places, since, if just one piece of the map falls into the wrong hands, all is lost.

Off go the hunters on their trails and, with luck, they all end up back with the Boffin at roughly the same time, bearing their bits of the map. The Dictator spends most of his time rushing about chasing hunters and, if any of them are thick enough to get caught, extracting information from them and exacting punishments of varying degrees. He can exercise some control over the game's progress by deliberately going out to delay a hunter who is getting too far ahead of the rest. He never actually gets his hands on a bit of the map.

When the map has been assembled, the Dictator retires, hissing vengeance and the Boffin distributes rewards to all the hunters. The Boffin then also retires and the hunters go on to another game or collapse exhausted.

If you have a ready source of outside people who would like to play a part in your hunt, you can give the baddie a couple of henchmen and you can have some more people on the good guy's side, perhaps holding vital clues. If you do this, one of the good people could also be mobile, which would give the hunters the added difficulty of finding him before being able to get a vital clue out of him.

This kind of hunt can have any number of variations, depending on the age and number of your hunters, the baddies you decide to play against and the time you have to prepare it. They are tremendous fun, with many hilarious and exciting moments.

PARTIES

PARTIES

Tired of the same old parties you get everywhere? Bored with *Musical Chairs* and *Pass the Parcel*? Seen the same old magic tricks so often that you know how they are done? If this is you, then it is time for you to make your own party different and exciting.

Parties can be the greatest fun, both for your guests and, just as important, for you. In fact, if you enjoy organizing your own party and playing the games, the chances are that your guests are having a great time too. I have played many of the games in this book again and again at parties all over the country – with wizards and witches, with masked villains, with cut-throat pirates and with horrifying ghouls and ghost-ies – and enjoyed them tremendously each time. Of course, there has been the odd occasion when a party has teetered on the brink of disaster, but somehow everything always came out all right in the end. There was the village hall, booked for the party but firmly locked up and the key gone missing; sudden downpours at outdoor parties; missed trains; halls promised to be 'huge' turning out to be the size of a shoe-box; even, once, a sudden influx of French children, none of whom spoke a word of English, which put a terrible strain on our feeble command of the French language as we struggled to translate rules!

There is no need at all for your party to be an elaborate and expensive occasion. Indeed, the best parties are often the simplest. Using the games in this book and the ideas in this section, you will be able to put together a shoestring party that will amaze and delight your friends, an occasion that will be remembered for a long time.

Invitations

Choose a day, a place and a time for your party. Make a list of the people you want to invite, bearing in mind the space you have available. It is important to invite people of roughly the same age, since a three-year-old is unlikely to enjoy the kind of party you would organize for a nine-year-old. There is also no point in inviting fifty friends to a party to be held in your living room, if there is really only room for twenty to sit round in a circle. If you are having an outdoor party, it is worth while having a room inside to fall back on if it pours with rain on the day. Decide how long you want your party to last. If it is going to be an indoor party, two hours is probably long enough, though you should allow more time if you are planning an elaborate tea as well. An outdoor party could go on a bit longer, especially if you are planning a treasure hunt.

One easy way to make your party different and more exciting is to make it a special party – a Witches' Coven, a Pirate Raid, a Beggars' Banquet, a Villains' Feast, a Wild Things' Rumpus, a Hat Party, a Masked Masquerade or a Ghostly Gathering – inviting your friends to come suitably dressed.

Write out your invitations carefully on cards or paper, making sure that you remember to add your name and address, the date and the time of the party (both the starting and the finishing time). Don't forget to put R.S.V.P. somewhere on them too, so that your friends know that they should let you know if they can come or not. If you are having a Villains' Feast, say so in huge, gruesome letters; perhaps you could also decorate the invitations with a dagger dripping blood or with villains cut out of comics or magazines. If you have got time and aren't inviting a large number of people, you could even cut letters and words out of newspapers to make your Villains' invitations look like ransom notes.

Send or deliver your invitations at least three weeks before the party so that your friends know about it in good time and don't plan anything else for that day. Keep a list of who you have invited, so that you can tick off the names as they reply.

Preparation

Start preparing your party about a week in advance. By this time, you should have a good idea of how many people are coming, so you can sit down and work out a list of games you want to play. Start with a rough list, writing the games down as they occur to you, and make a note of how long you think each of them will take. If you are having a two-hour indoor party, you will need about an hour and forty minutes' worth of games to be on the safe side.

Have a good look at the list of games you have written down and think about the order in which you would like to play them. Start a new list, allowing ten to fifteen minutes at the beginning for all your friends to turn up and allowing for a break for tea or refreshments about half-way through. This leaves you with two patches of time to fill with games. Try to start each patch with a quick game that involves everybody, like *Stand Up, Sit Down, Shooting Fish* or *A What?* After that, try to alternate games that involve everybody with those that only involve two at a time. You should also try to get a good mix of quiet games in between noisy or riotous games, to give everybody a chance to catch their breath. If you have a heavy tea, perhaps the second patch should begin with a few quiet games before pulling the stops out on the noisy ones.

Assuming that you have invited roughly twenty people for two hours, your party plan will now look something like this:

3.00 Party starts – people arrive
3.15 Games: *Stand Up, Sit down* (3 mins.)
　　　　　　 Shoeing Horses (10 mins.)

       Who Has the Ball? (10 mins.)
       Rabbits (10 mins.)
       Fishtails (10 mins.)
       King Silence (5 mins.)
4.00 Tea
4.10 Games: *Shooting Fish* (3 mins.)
             Earth, Air, Water (10 mins.)
             Chinball (5 mins.)
             Cops and Robbers (10 mins.)
             Guided Rockets (5 mins.)
             All Change (10 mins.)
             Locomotion (10 mins.)
             The Mummy Game (5 mins.)
5.00 Party ends

An outdoor party takes much the same shape as an indoor party, unless you are planning a treasure hunt, in which case you might decide to play a couple of short games to start with, then have the treasure hunt and aim to finish with a later tea. Then play a few, longish games until it is time to go home.

Once you have your plan, you should start getting together any bits and pieces that you might need for the games. Collect the stumps, bat and tennis ball from their various hiding-places; collect yoghurt pots; make your blindfolds (if you are planning to use headscarves, test them out for size, since some are too small to tie satisfactorily); make your fishtails; and buy what you want for tea.

If you are having a special party, you can add to the atmosphere by changing the names of the games you are going to play, so that *Cops and Robbers* could become *Two Witches and a Cat* for a Coven, *Vampires and a Victim* for a Villains' Feast or *Catching a Ghost* for a Ghostly Gathering.

Starting Games

When you are having a party, there is always an awkward ten minutes or so right at the beginning, when a few people have arrived, some are just arriving and some are yet to get there. You are faced with the problem of giving your early friends something to keep them amused and interested while waiting for the rest to turn up. You don't want the early arrivals to be bored rigid with nothing to do, nor do you want to start on the main party games until everybody has got there. The ideal thing is to prepare some short pencil and paper games that can be going on at the beginning. The *Feely Box* and *Smelly Boxes* work well here, as do *Adverts* and *Cook Up a Story*. You could always prepare *Picture Pieces* too, though you will be too busy to open the front door yourself. If your party is for about twenty people, *Picture Pieces* and one other game will probably just fill the gap nicely before everybody is there.

Do's and Don'ts

DO make sure that you know the rules for all the games you are going to play. If you are not sure of them, try them out on unsuspecting friends or family some time before the party.

DO make sure that you have all the equipment you need for each game ready to hand and ready to use. A successful party is one where the fun never stops, so you should try to move smoothly from one game into the next, avoiding tiresome delays.

DO keep your list of games on you throughout the party. It is very easy to forget your planned order or even a whole game in the heat of the moment. If you have got the list with you, you probably won't need to refer to it, but if you haven't got it with you, you are bound to wish you had!

DON'T let a game run too much over the time you had given it, even if it seems to be going well. There are two reasons for this. First, if you run a lot over on one game, it will put your plan out and you will have to improvise fast. Second, it is usually a good idea to leave a game when it is going well. That way you can be sure that no one is getting bored.

Tea

If your party is being run on a shoestring, don't bother with a big, elaborate party tea. Orange squash and a selection of biscuits is fine for a short break in the middle, just enough to quench a thirst from rushing around – and who ever turns down biscuits?

If you do decide to organize a more elaborate tea, be careful not to let it drag on otherwise some people will be finished and getting bored and you will find yourself without enough time to finish your prepared games.

Prizes

On the whole, it should not be necessary to award prizes for the games you are playing, since they are fun enough in themselves. However, if you are having a special party and people have taken a lot of trouble to dress up as Villains, Ghosts or Pirates, you might feel that you would like to give the best one or two a token prize as some small reward for the effort they have made. If you do decide to award a prize, make the decision quickly, keep the prize small, make a minimum of fuss and move swiftly on to something else, since by awarding one person a prize, you are, of course, disappointing all the rest.

INDEX OF GAMES

All The Year Round
Toni Arthur

A colourful collection of activities to do throughout the year. Month by month, here are ideas for things to make and do appropriate to the month.

Cars, Boats, Trains and Planes
Castles, Churches and Houses
Alan Jamieson

Two books designed to help children recognize objects and buildings they see when travelling about the countryside and towns, on holiday or in a car.

Houdini's Book of Magic
Ben Hamilton

A fascinating selection of 'magic' as performed by the great Houdini himself. Starting with simple tricks requiring few props and little preparation, the book progresses in difficulty and lets you in on the secrets of Houdini's most famous illusions. A must for all budding magicians.

Heard about the Puffin Club?

... it's a way of finding out more about Puffin books and authors, of winning prizes (in competitions), sharing jokes, a secret code, and perhaps seeing your name in print! When you join you get a copy of our magazine, *Puffin Post*, sent to you four times a year, a badge and a membership book.

For details of subscription and an application form, send a stamped addressed envelope to:

The Puffin Club Dept A
Penguin Books Limited
Bath Road
Harmondsworth
Middlesex UB7 ODA

and if you live in Australia, please write to:

The Australian Puffin Club
Penguin Books Australia Limited
P.O. Box 257
Ringwood
Victoria 3134